McGraw-Hill's

CAREERS FOR

HISTORY BUFFS

& Others Who Learn from the Past

Careers for You Series

McGRAW-HILL'S

CAREERS FOR

HISTORY BUFFS

& Others Who Learn from the Past

BLYTHE CAMENSON

THIRD EDITION

New York Chicago San Francisco Lisbon London Madrid Mexico City
Milan New Delhi San Juan Seoul Singapore Sydney Toronto

The McGraw·Hill Companies

Library of Congress Cataloging-in-Publication Data

Camenson, Blythe.
    Careers for history buffs & others who learn from the past / by Blythe
Camenson — 3rd ed.
       p. cm. — (McGraw-Hill careers for you series)
    Rev. ed. of: Careers for history buffs & others who learn from the past. 2nd ed.
©2002.
    Includes bibliographical references.
    ISBN 0-07-154537-9 (alk. paper)
    1. United States—History—Vocational guidance. 2. Canada—History—
Vocational guidance. 3. History—Vocational guidance—United States.
4. History—Vocational guidance—Canada. I. Camenson, Blythe. Careers for
history buffs & others who learn from the past. II. Title.

E175.C33 2008
902′.373—dc22   2008022920

1 2 3 4 5 6 7 8 9 10 11 12 13 14 15 16 17 18 19 20 DOC/DOC 0 9 8

ISBN 978-0-07-154537-2
MHID   0-07-154537-9

McGraw-Hill books are available at special quantity discounts to use as premiums
and sales promotions or for use in corporate training programs. To contact a
representative, please visit the Contact Us pages at www.mhprofessional.com.

*To all the people who came before us, for
without them we would have no history
and no avid interest to consume us*

Contents

A Word from the Author   ix

Acknowledgments   xi

CHAPTER ONE   **Jobs for History Buffs**   I

CHAPTER TWO   **Living History Museums**
Making History Come Alive   II

CHAPTER THREE   **The National Park Service**
Interpreting Our National Treasures   29

CHAPTER FOUR   **History Museums**
Displaying the Past   41

CHAPTER FIVE   **Jobs for Structure Lovers**
Preserving the Past   61

CHAPTER SIX   **Jobs in Historical Societies**
Explaining the Past   71

CHAPTER SEVEN   **Jobs for Diggers**
Uncovering the Past   81

CHAPTER EIGHT   **Writing and Photography**
Documenting the Past   99

CHAPTER NINE   **The Self-Employed History Buff**
                Profiting from the Past   109

CHAPTER TEN   **Scholarly, Academic, and Scientific
                Jobs for History Buffs**   129

APPENDIX A: **Associations, Halls of Fame,
                Societies, and Museums**   135

APPENDIX B: **Living History Museums**   149

APPENDIX C: **National Park Service
                Regional Offices**   153

APPENDIX D: **Further Reading**   157

A Word from the Author

....

Almost a decade ago, while interviewing the thirty or so professionals profiled in this book, I was struck again and again by the one thing all these diverse people had in common. From tour guides working for an hourly wage to chiefs and directors at the top of the salary scale, all of them unequivocally expressed love for the work they're doing.

At the time I thought it was rare to find so many people satisfied with their professions. Now, a decade later, in updating this book, I was able to track down all of the people featured within these pages. With a few exceptions, most have stayed at the same jobs or in the same line of work, still loving them as much every day as they did then. Those who have left their jobs have moved into self-employment but still maintain contact with their previous employers, several of them as consultants or individual contractors.

I thought so then, and I still feel that way now: there is something unique and wonderful about the field of history—and the people who enter it.

Salaries have hardly budged in the intervening years, and few if any of the history buffs within these pages have become famous, but they are all happy. My guess is if you pursue a career in this diverse field, you will be, too.

Acknowledgments

The author would like to thank the following history lovers for providing information about their careers:

Don Albro	Former Director of Historic Sites
	Joseph Smith Historic Site
	Nauvoo, Illinois
Patricia Baker	Former Wardrobe and Textiles Manager
	Plimoth Plantation
	Plymouth, Massachusetts
Peter Benton	Restoration Architect
	John Milner Associates, Inc.
	West Chester, Pennsylvania
Prudy Taylor Board	Publisher
	Prudy's Press
	Fort Myers, Florida
Jeff Donnelly	Volunteer Tour Guide
	Miami Design Preservation League
	Miami Beach, Florida
Tom Doyle	Carriage Tour Operator
	Palmetto Carriage Works, Ltd.
	Charleston, South Carolina
John Fleckner	Chief Archivist
	National Museum of American History,
	Smithsonian Institution
	Washington, D.C.

Mark Fortenberry   Former Curator of Structures
Nantucket Historical Association
Nantucket, Massachusetts

Jeremy Fried   Character Interpreter
Colonial Williamsburg Foundation
Williamsburg, Virginia

Tom Gerhardt   Interpretive Artisan: Cooper
Plimoth Plantation
Plymouth, Massachusetts

Hank Grasso   Exhibit Designer
National Museum of American History,
Smithsonian Institution
Washington, D.C.

Kristin Kuckelman   Field Anthropologist
Crow Canyon Archaeological Center
Cortez, Colorado

Kendra Lambert   Former Student Intern
National Museum of American History,
Smithsonian Institution
Washington, D.C.

Michael Larsen   Literary Agent/Author
San Francisco, California

Antoinette Lee   Historian
National Register of Historic Places
Washington, D.C.

Deb Mason   Pottery Supervisor, Crafts Center
Plimoth Plantation
Plymouth, Massachusetts

Charles McGovern   Curator
National Museum of American History,
Smithsonian Institution
Washington, D.C.

George Neary   Former Administrative Director/
Information Officer
Miami Design Preservation League
Miami Beach, Florida

Cookie O'Brien	Columnist
	Historic St. Augustine Preservation
	Board
	St. Augustine, Florida
Adam Perl	Antique Dealer
	Pastimes
	Ithaca, New York
Elizabeth Pomada	Literary Agent/Author
	San Francisco, California
Joel Pontz	Former Supervisor of Interpretive
	Artisans
	Plimoth Plantation
	Plymouth, Massachusetts
Mary Ptak	Vintage Clothing Specialist
	Jezebel
	Fort Lauderdale, Florida
Jim Ridolfi	Auctioneer
	Aspon Trading Company
	Troy, Pennsylvania
Roger and Mary	Former Proprietors
Schmidt	18 Gardner Street Inn
	Nantucket, Massachusetts
Jeremy Slavitz	Public Programs Coordinator
	Nantucket Historical Association
	Nantucket, Massachusetts
Carolyn Travers	Director of Research
	Plimoth Plantation
	Plymouth, Massachusetts
Gordie Wilson	Superintendent
	Castillo de San Marcos National
	Monument
	St. Augustine, Florida

CHAPTER ONE

Jobs for History Buffs

The United States, which might be considered a young country by some of the rest of the world's standards, is nevertheless a land steeped in history. Throughout the country there are thousands of historic homes and public buildings, restored and reconstructed villages—even entire cities—to explore.

North America is also rich with relics of past civilizations and past visitors and conquerors—early Native Americans, Vikings, Spanish and Dutch and French settlers, Pilgrims and Puritans, and pioneers of the Wild West, to name just a few.

Of course, many history buffs don't limit their interests to North America. There's a whole world out there—Europe and Asia, Africa and South America, and Australia—with millennia of cultures and events to examine.

What Makes a History Buff?

History buffs are fascinated by events, places, and people from the past. There are armchair historians, devouring innumerable biographies and researched accounts, as well as hands-on types who are out in the field digging for artifacts, exploring the lanes and roadways our ancestors once walked, or fighting to preserve historic buildings and monuments.

History buffs possess qualities as diverse as the areas of interest to explore. Some are thrilled by the discoveries of research or are collectors and catalogers by nature. They might enjoy working with their hands, re-creating early American crafts with a potter's wheel or hand plane, or duplicating period clothing. To some, preserving and restoring the lines and structures of historic houses and buildings hold great interest.

Others love the smell of old books and paper and spend most of their time in libraries or government or private archives. Still others enjoy sharing their knowledge through talks and presentations or through the written word. They've found a niche working with the public as tour guides or information officers or writing articles and booklets for publication.

Among the traits history buffs do have in common are an insatiable curiosity and a love of the relics, events, people, and places of the past.

The Employment Outlook

Where once settings in which history buffs could find employment were limited to a few museums and libraries, there are now thousands of new opportunities across the country. Public interest in preserving our American heritage has grown tremendously in recent years. Every state has several departments devoted to different aspects of its local history. Most major cities, and even small towns, support a variety of historical societies and preservation boards. More and more historic buildings are nominated each year for inclusion on the National Register; many of these sites are operated as historic house museums that are open to the public.

New job titles have been added to the list that was once limited to curators, librarians, and teachers. The field of history is now open to all sorts of professionals, including restoration specialists, designers, planners, financiers, audience advocates, information specialists, genealogists, and many more.

Although the competition in some sectors is stiff, and funding always seems to lag behind public demand, a persistent history buff can get her or his foot in the door through volunteering or participating in a student internship.

Heaven-Sent Jobs for History Buffs

Job-hunting history buffs dream of finding a position where their skills and interests can be combined. Would any of these help-wanted ads send you racing to the post office to mail off your resume?

Information Officer. Historic site preservation board has opening for officer to disseminate information to the public. Good writing skills necessary. Bilingual, Spanish/English, a plus.

Researcher. Author seeks experienced researcher for project documenting restored Victorian houses. Must be willing to travel.

Tour Guide. Outgoing person with good communication skills needed to guide special-interest groups through American history museum in Washington, D.C.

Potter. Wanted: fine-arts major familiar with or willing to learn seventeenth-century crafts techniques for demonstrating at living history museum.

Dig Site Assistant. Position open for energetic student or recent graduate at major archaeological dig site in New Mexico. Duties include cleaning and recording discovered artifacts.

Requirements

Required qualifications vary depending on the job. Although many employers prefer their applicants to have a bachelor's or higher degree in history or a related field, not all do. Theater

majors often make excellent tour guides and character interpreters. Parks and recreation majors are often welcomed with the
National Park Service.

Many jobs discussed in this book don't require a college degree.
In some situations, the following qualifications are more important: experience, extensive knowledge of a particular time period
or region, the ability to communicate with diverse groups of people, and good writing and research skills.

Earnings

Salaries vary widely from position to position but are relatively
low, as are most pay scales for education-related fields. Factors
such as the source of funding or the region of the country often
affect salary levels more than the complexity of the job or the level
of the candidate's education and experience.

Some history jobs pay only hourly wages; others follow the federal government's General Service (GS) scale. A tour guide might
earn $8 to $12 an hour, an information officer perhaps $32,000 to
$40,000 a year, a restoration architect $56,000 to $62,000.

Most jobs provide benefits such as health insurance, sick leave,
vacations, and retirement plans. But all those interviewed on the
pages to come stressed that financial rewards were not the main
reason or, for some, even a consideration, in pursuing their chosen professions. For many, even the drawback of low pay was far
outweighed by the satisfaction of doing work they love.

Choosing a Profession

There are thousands of jobs related to history. With so many areas
of history to explore, how do you know which avenue would be
right for you? Take a look at the chart that follows. Find your
interests and skills, and then look across to identify some related

career options. You'll see that many of the job titles combine more than one interest. A short description of some of these jobs follows the chart, and more in-depth discussions will be found in the chapters to come.

Interests and Skills	Job Titles
Old houses	Restoration Architect, Architectural Historian, Curator of Structures, Preservationist, Curator, Exhibit Designer, Historic Interiors Specialist
Working with your hands	Furniture Restorer, Restoration Architect, Curator of Structures, Archaeologist, Artisan, Archivist, Costumer, Antiques Dealer, Refinisher, Exhibit Designer
Working in the arts	Artist, Historic Musician, Photographer, Camera Operator, Lighting and Sound Specialist, Historic Dance Choreographer or Performer
Finding out information	Historian, Researcher, Internet Research Specialist, Archaeologist, Archivist, Genealogist, Curator
Working with the public	Character Interpreter, Tour Guide, Information Officer, Park Ranger, Historic Inn Operator, Historic Crafts Demonstrator, Public Relations Representative, Educator, Auctioneer
Writing	Information Officer, Public Relations Representative, Historian, Script Writer, Curator, Archaeologist, Book Author
Working outdoors	Archaeologist, Restoration Architect, Character Interpreter, Curator of Structures, Park Ranger, Auctioneer

Job categories are as varied as their locations. The following paragraphs give a brief overview of the many jobs discussed in this book.

Jobs for Historians

The term *historian* covers a large range of career options and job settings. In general, historians study, assess, and interpret the recent and the distant past to determine what happened and why. They examine court documents, diaries, letters, and newspaper accounts; they interview individuals and study archaeological evidence. They conduct research, write, teach, evaluate, and make recommendations.

Historians work in schools and universities, in libraries and museums, in government offices, and in private enterprises.

Jobs in Living History Museums

Do you have a good memory (and good vision)? Do you like to pore over old documents researching lives of America's ancestors? How about a flair for improvisation and the dramatic? Can you think fast on your feet? Or work with your hands? These qualities, and more, could land you a job as a researcher, character interpreter, or craft worker at Colonial Williamsburg or Plimoth Plantation, two of the many living history museums that are maintained in the United States.

Jobs with the National Park Service

Although many people picture park rangers for the National Park Service as being concerned with fire prevention, nature, and conservation, there is another category of ranger that would be of interest to history buffs. Interpretation park rangers, both men and women, work at the more than two hundred historic sites and national monuments throughout the country. This division of rangers is devoted to preserving and explaining the past.

Jobs in History Museums

Positions in history museums range from directors and curators to educators and designers. Depending upon the position, responsibilities could include administration, fund-raising, researching, cataloging, collecting, preserving, restoring, displaying, explaining, and guarding.

Jobs in Architectural History and Restoration

Lovers of the architectural styles and structures of the past are moved to study them, restore and renovate, reproduce, or preserve and protect them. They often work with their hands, creating drawings or lifting beams and sanding wood trim.

Jobs with Historical Societies

People who work for historical societies and on preservation boards enjoy teamwork, serving on committees, and educating the public—and they are not afraid to fight for a cause they believe in. Through the work of dedicated preservationists across the country, thousands of historic buildings, even entire districts, have been saved from the wrecking ball. Many of these sites have since achieved national recognition.

Jobs in Archaeology

Can you pay attention to detail and perform delicate, painstaking tasks? Do you dream of traveling to Egypt or Israel, to Peru or Turkey? As an archaeologist or assistant, your work could take you around the world, literally uncovering the past, one grain of sand at a time.

Jobs in Genealogy

Genealogists act as detectives to the past, tracing missing persons, filling in the holes in family histories. They interview older family members; visit courthouses, cemeteries, and libraries; and spend hours poring over diaries, old newspaper accounts, marriage licenses, and birth and death certificates.

Jobs for Communicators

Historical films, videos, pageants, and presentations require writers, directors, actors, announcers, narrators, and musicians, as well as costumers, makeup artists, scene designers, and construction people. If you have a talent for writing, know how to handle a camera, or have other theatrical talents, you may want to work with words and pictures to share your love of past cultures, places, and events of historical interest.

Interactive materials, including websites and computer games, newsletters, books, magazines, brochures and pamphlets, and other electronic and print materials provide jobs for computer scientists, historical writers, illustrators, photographers, designers, and others.

The Self-Employed History Buff

Want to be your own boss? There are many businesses and sidelines into which a history buff can venture, including the following examples: running a historic inn; dealing in antiques; creating, promoting, and operating your own tour company; restoring and selling vintage clothing. The list is limited only by your imagination.

Other Jobs for History Buffs

Education, art history, landscape archaeology, and the "ologies"—anthropology, paleontology, and geology—and are just a few more career paths that dedicated history buffs with an academic leaning can investigate.

The Job Hunt

Although many history buffs are able to find employment in their own hometowns—in local historical societies or historic house museums—chances are you'll have to relocate to broaden your opportunities. If you have a spot in mind where you'd like to work, a phone call or an introductory letter or e-mail sent with your resume is a good way to start. If you would like some more ideas on possible locations, there are several directories listed in the coming chapters and in the appendices that can lead you to interesting destinations.

Since many sites are state or federally operated, you might have to obtain a special application through state or federal offices. Some private employers, however, such as the Colonial Williamsburg Foundation, expect job hopefuls to apply in person. The foundation regularly posts openings and operates a job hotline with recorded messages.

Many historical organizations and professional associations produce monthly or quarterly newsletters with job listings and upcoming internships and fellowships. Some key addresses, as well as suggested further readings, have been provided for you throughout the following chapters and in the appendices.

Don't forget the Internet, which, these days, has become one of the premier resources for job hunting. Fire up any search engine and enter key words such as history, jobs, museums, curators, and so on. A well-defined search will bring you to many interesting and helpful websites.

Also, visit the websites of the professional associations listed in Appendix A. Many of these websites offer specific career information and list job openings.

CHAPTER TWO

Living History Museums

Making History Come Alive

Most people living in the United States and in many parts of Canada and Europe have visited at least one living history museum. These attractive restorations of historical homes, commercial buildings, villages, towns, and even ghost towns are fun to visit and make good family excursions.

A living history museum provides a setting in which the vibrant, active day-to-day life of a particular time period has been authentically re-created. Once you step through the gates, you leave the present behind. The houses and public buildings are restored originals or thoroughly researched reproductions. Interiors are outfitted with period furniture, cookware, bed linens, and tablecloths. Peek under a bed and you might even find a two- or three-hundred-year-old mousetrap.

"Residents" of the restored setting wear the clothing of the period and discuss their dreams and concerns with visitors as they go about their daily tasks. If you were to stop a costumed gentleman passing by and ask where the nearest McDonald's is, he wouldn't seem to have any idea what you were talking about—unless he thought to direct you to a neighbor's farm. He might even do so using the dialect of his home country.

Colonial Williamsburg in Virginia and Plimoth Plantation in Massachusetts are just two well-known examples of the many living history museums that thrive in the United States today, and they receive hundreds of thousands of visitors each year. The addresses and websites of many others are provided for your interest and reference in Appendix B.

Many of the living history museums are large enterprises that provide various kinds of employment for professional and entry-level workers in a wide range of categories. These include, but are not limited to, actors and character interpreters, authentic period crafters of different kinds, presenters, costumers, guides, and researchers.

Living history is expensive to create, and many sites are state or federally funded. Additional support may be received through admission tickets and private donations. Colonial Williamsburg, with its beautifully and painstakingly restored colonial-era village, falls into this latter category.

Close-Up: Colonial Williamsburg

Visitors to Colonial Williamsburg meet historic figures, witness events, and participate in the daily lives of the people who helped bring about American independence.

For eighty-one years, from 1699 to 1780 (though only die-hard history buffs need to remember the dates), Williamsburg was the thriving capital of Virginia, one of the original thirteen American colonies. After the American Revolution, when the capital was moved to Richmond, Williamsburg began a decline that lasted 146 years. It became a sleepy southern town with crumbling roads and buildings, overgrown gardens, and only a distant memory of patriots and prosperity. In 1926, with his love of American history and a belief that anything was possible, John D. Rockefeller Jr. began the Colonial Williamsburg restoration project to return this once-important city to its former glory.

After more than seventy years of work, nearly a hundred original eighteenth-century and early nineteenth-century structures have been completely restored, and more than five hundred others have been reconstructed on original foundations. This physical construction was undertaken only after extensive archaeological and historical investigation.

The principal thoroughfare in Williamsburg is the Duke of Gloucester Street, which began as nothing more than a winding horse path flanked by a tavern and a few shops and houses. Then, in 1693, with the establishment of the College of William and Mary (North America's second-oldest university, Harvard being the oldest) at the western end and the impressive capitol building at the far eastern end, the street was widened and became the busy center of daily activity. Today it is closed to traffic, though an occasional horse-drawn carriage or stagecoach clatters by. Eighteenth-century shops and houses still stand, shaded by beautiful old trees lining the hard-packed dirt walkways.

These buildings are not just empty symbols of a bygone era, however. Many of the homes shelter permanent residents—employees of the Colonial Williamsburg Foundation—or act as inns to house the many visitors who come every year. Those that are open to the public are filled with the same artifacts, activities, and people that made up daily life in colonial times.

Character Interpreter

The most visible living history museum employees are the scores of men and women decked out in authentic period costumes. They can be found waiting inside the buildings or walking through the grounds, and although they might seem to be there just for decoration—or photo opportunities, as they are sometimes called—most are trained researchers, actors, and presenters. A select group of these staff members use first person interpretation or role-playing to explain their places in history. They are called character interpreters or "people of the past." They are in actuality skilled social historians who have researched early residents and assumed their roles.

In Williamsburg, you can follow Mrs. Powell about town as this eighteenth-century housewife does her errands, or visit the Powell House and speak with Mr. Powell, the prominent Williamsburg builder. You can spend the afternoon in the capitol yard listening to colonial gentlemen discussing events of the day or converse with Mr. Samuel Henley, an eighteenth-century professor at the College of William and Mary, and learn about the values and traditions of his time. You can eavesdrop on young gentlemen as they prepare for college and share their expectations and concerns for the future.

Visiting children can join a costumed interpreter to explore the interaction of colonial family life, youth apprenticeships, education, work, and leisure time.

At Plimoth Plantation, you can listen to seventeenth-century Goodwife Cook plan her day or share tidbits of gossip with Governor Bradford's sister-in-law. John Alden is there, making barrels in his one-room cottage or helping other villagers erect a new house. Not too far away, seventeenth-century sailors swab the decks or repair the lines on the *Mayflower II*, while passengers discuss their worries about surviving the first winter in the New World.

What It's Like to Be a Character Interpreter

The job of a character interpreter is explained by Jeremy Fried, who, in addition to his position as manager of character interpreters at Williamsburg, has been interpreting the role of James Hubard, a colonial lawyer, off and on for more than ten years. Jeremy said of his work:

"My character spends most of his time in chambers, a fair-sized room in the courthouse, with a table in the middle seating twelve people. I sit down with a law book and quill and paper, and people come in and chat. But I don't work from a prepared script—that's what makes this form of interpretation different from other forms of living history.

"A character interpreter, often with the help of our various research departments, examines the life of an eighteenth-century person by reading available documentation—personal letters, letters to the editor, newspapers. From this we can make inferences about their lives and what their beliefs were. As accurately as possible, we portray their ideas, social knowledge, and political opinions.

"Visitors ask questions about how 'I' became a lawyer, about my family, about life in general in the eighteenth century. I've had people stay with me for one-and-a-half to two hours. This gets to be a bit of a challenge to stay in character. But I enjoy it."

Qualifications. Jeremy stressed that the most important qualifications an applicant should possess are the ability to communicate with people, a pleasing personality, and an inquisitive mind. These requirements generally hold true for all living history museums throughout the country.

Jeremy further explained: "Of course, the foundation prefers people with a history major, but the flip side is, unless you've done your master's thesis on colonial Virginian society, you're still going to have to do the research. You could have only a GED but still be able to formulate new ideas and coordinate information.

"We have a number of folks with history degrees, but we also have a retired florist and a former petty officer in the navy. It's a mixed bag of backgrounds. I have a degree in theater from the American Academy of Dramatic Arts in New York."

Jeremy added one other qualification: "An applicant would have to be willing to accept a pretty low pay range."

Salaries. A full-time entry-level character interpreter earns only an hourly wage, from minimum wage to around $12, which varies with experience. But although it's an hourly wage, employees are given full benefits. Most contracts are for a ten-month period. A percentage of employees are laid off for two months during the winter, then rehired.

Offsetting the low salaries, Jeremy noted, is that the people really enjoy working for the foundation. "It's a nice work environment," he said. "The biggest stress is being hospitable to folks on vacation, and that's not a bad situation."

Salaries vary from site to site, of course, but most generally follow the same range offered in Williamsburg.

Hours. Most full-time employees put in an eight-hour day. At least four of those hours are spent in the characters' natural environment in chambers, in class at the college, or in their shops or homes. The rest of the time is spent moving around town, chatting with visitors, becoming a photo opportunity.

Ample time during the week is also allocated for research or to produce facsimile newspapers in the winter months.

Character interpreters at Plimoth Plantation attend to all the necessary tasks to keep the village thriving. They work in the fields, care for the farm animals, which have been especially back-bred to resemble breeds as they were about three hundred years ago, and build new houses or repair existing ones.

Advancement. A national association of interpreters has been formed to let people know that interpreting history is a highly specialized skill. Opportunities occasionally come up to advance, but perhaps not in the interpretive roles that the actors enjoy most. "Right now," Jeremy admitted, "the only way to advance is to get out of interpreting and into management."

How to Apply. The application process for a job as an interpreter is relatively simple. A quick telephone call or letter will have an application on its way to you. Many websites include employment lines to tell you what positions are currently available. See Appendix B for more information and ways to contact the living history museums listed.

Presenter

Jobs for presenters are much more numerous throughout the country than are character interpretation positions. Presenters differ from character interpreters in that most of them work from prepared scripts. Here, acting ability is more important than research and ad-libbing skills.

Presenters generally reenact moments from history—a court scene, the Boston Tea Party, a fife-and-drum corps march—or other aspects of life in the historic site's particular period. Sometimes, because enough information is not available for a particular place or people—the native people in seventeenth-century Plymouth, for example—a character interpreter would not be able to authentically take on a first-person role. Then presenters would explain to visitors what is known about the time in the third person. Presenters usually perform outfitted in authentic costumes.

Salaries for presenters are generally low, and employment can often be seasonal, but the rewards of discussing your favorite place or time in history often compensate for the downsides.

Costumer

Most living history museums employ professional costumers to keep their character interpreters and presenters outfitted in authentic period clothing. Costumers generally work behind the scenes, reproducing the apparel the average inhabitant would have worn.

What It's Like to Be a Costumer at Plimoth Plantation

One costumer, Patricia Baker, was wardrobe and textiles manager and then became an occasional consultant at Plimoth Plantation, a living history museum that has re-created the year 1627, seven years after the arrival of the *Mayflower* at Plymouth Rock.

Patricia's office and work space occupied a section of a converted dairy barn on the grounds of the museum. The atmosphere was that of a cozy living room with lots of shelves, fabrics draped here and there, sewing machines and rocking chairs, a large cutting table, garment racks, and a radio. Patricia discussed her former job:

"The department I worked for makes clothes that are common to what the middle class would have worn. It provides interpreters with enough clothing so they can dress authentically from the skin out. They don't even have to wear modern underwear if they don't want to.

"The basic undergarment for both men and women is a shift. It's a long, linen, T-shaped garment that reaches to the knees. Over that, the men wear breeches and a doublet, a close-fitting jacket that comes to just above the waist. The breeches are tied into the jacket by laces.

"Women wear a plain corset over the shift. It gives them a smooth, cone-shaped look. Next come a number of petticoats and skirts and a padded roll to enhance their hips. Waistlines are raised and meet in a point.

"The costumers use wool and linen and a little cotton, all naturally dyed, and try to duplicate the same materials used in the seventeenth century, as well as the same construction techniques. Much of the sewing is done by hand.

"They also make all the household furnishings that are used for display in the various exhibits. These are the seventeenth-century equivalents to what we have in the twentieth century: sheets, pillowcases (called pillow beres), feather and straw beds, paneled bed curtains, tablecloths, napkins, and cupboard cloths.

"Maintaining and repairing existing costumes and furnishings are also part of the duties, as well as conducting as much research as possible to keep the creations accurate for the particular time period.

"Because there are so few surviving garments—conditions were very harsh in those early years—costumers look to different sources: paintings, engravings, woodcuts, written descriptions, wills, inventories, diaries, and plays.

"They also study the few remaining garments on display in different museums through our extensive slide collection of styles and techniques. Most of those museums are in England—the Victoria and Albert Museum or the Museum of Costume in Bath, for example. The clothing seems to have had a better survival rate over there."

Background. Patricia graduated from the Massachusetts College of Art in 1976 with a bachelor of fine arts degree in crafts. Her concentration was in fabrics and fibers. After graduation, she immediately began work at Plimoth Plantation as a character interpreter. She joined the wardrobe department in 1985 and became its head the following year. She then went to work with the Costume Society of America and still occasionally served as a consultant for Plimoth Plantation.

How to Get Started. The wardrobe department at Plimoth Plantation is a small one, currently employing only four workers. Other larger living history museums, such as Colonial Williamsburg, need more people. A good way to get a foot in the door is to apply for an apprenticeship, internship, or work-study position.

Salaries. On average, a new graduate just starting out could expect an annual salary in the $23,000 to $34,000 range, depending on the location and available funding.

The Historic Trades

Most living history museums employ skilled artisans to demonstrate early crafts and trades. Some of these artisans perform in the first person, playing the role of a particular character of the time. Others wear twentieth-century clothing and discuss their crafts from a modern perspective.

In the stores and workshops lining the Duke of Gloucester and Francis Streets in Colonial Williamsburg, you will find harness makers, milliners, tailors, needleworkers, silversmiths, apothecaries, candle makers, bookbinders, printers, and wig makers. In the Pilgrim Village and Crafts Center at Plimoth Plantation, there are coopers, blacksmiths, joiners (cabinetmakers), potters, and basket makers and weavers.

In addition to giving demonstrations, artisans often produce many of the items used on display in the various exhibits. This includes the furniture, cookware, and even sometimes the actual buildings.

Interpretive Artisans at Plimoth Plantation

Most of the items the Pilgrims used in 1627 were brought with them on the *Mayflower* or imported later. Because the Pilgrim Village at Plimoth Plantation is time-specific to the year 1627, only those crafts that were practiced then are demonstrated there. In addition to their principal occupation as farmers, 1627 Pilgrims were coopers, blacksmiths, thatchers, and house builders. The interpretive artisans perform in costume and play the role of a designated Pilgrim documented to have lived in Plymouth during that year.

What It's Like to Be a Cooper at Plimoth Plantation

Tom Gerhardt interprets the character of one of the most famous Pilgrims, John Alden, a cooper who worked both inside a one-room cottage he shared with his wife and two children and outside in the adjoining yard. Tom talked about his job:

"I make barrels and other different-sized wooden containers, such as buckets and churns, while answering visitors' questions about life in seventeenth-century Plymouth.

"Although in Europe you could still find people practicing the craft as it once was done, there are only a few barrel makers in this country. Wooden barrels are made mostly for the wine and spirits industry, but now it's a mechanized craft using power tools and machinery. The finished product is the same as the old craft, but the method is different. We practice the craft as it was done in the 1600s, using only hand tools.

"In addition to my duties as an interpretive cooper, I am also responsible for general woodworking. I am one of several Pilgrims building a new house on the grounds.

"What I enjoy most about Plimoth Plantation is that there are a number of very creative and talented people here. If you're willing to do the work, you can learn a good deal for yourself, while at the same time you're educating the visitors.

"There are so many people who will help you—you can be inspired by what they're doing, and you have the time to explore and develop your skills."

Background. Tom's interest in history began as a small child. His father was a volunteer in charge of a small museum in Virginia, and he took the family on vacations all over the country visiting other museums. It was on one of these trips Tom first discovered Plimoth Plantation. Later, Tom took a few courses under a master cooper in Portsmouth, New Hampshire, and went to college for a couple of years, studying liberal arts and theater. He worked in the technical end of theater for a while but decided he wanted a change. Since he'd always been interested in the re-creation of history, in 1985 he came back to Plimoth Plantation and applied for a job as an interpreter, a role he very much enjoys.

What It's Like to Be a Joiner at Plimoth Plantation

Plimoth Plantation also operates the Crafts Center, where other seventeenth-century crafts are demonstrated. Potters, joiners, basket makers, weavers, and a gift shop share space in a converted carriage house. Artisans in the Crafts Center wear twentieth-century clothing and discuss the work from a modern viewpoint.

Joel Pontz was the supervisor of all interpretive artisans at Plimoth Plantation as well as character interpreter for a farmer, John Adams. He also demonstrated his joinery skills in the Crafts Center. He now does custom woodworking and occasionally completes contract work for Plimoth Plantation. Joel described his former job:

"I stepped back and forth between the seventeenth and the twentieth centuries. Several days a week I was in costume in the village as John Adams, picking my share of rutabagas or building small animal shelters or fences. On the other days I was in modern clothing in the Crafts Center, demonstrating joinery.

"Joiners were the principal furniture makers of the period, in the age before cabinetry. We used different kinds of saws and edged hand tools, such as axes, planes, gimlets, and augers, rather than power tools. If we wanted to reproduce the right texture or style, we had to be purists about it.

"In the Crafts Center, in front of the public or behind the scenes, we made furniture for the village—large cupboards, bedsteads, chairs, mousetraps, and children's toys. We didn't want to demonstrate any crafts in the village section of the museum that weren't practiced at the time. It would be anachronistic."

Background. Joel Pontz grew up near Plimoth Plantation and began as a volunteer Pilgrim after school and on weekends. In 1973, he became a full-time character interpreter. He learned his joinery skill on-site from the other staff members and the research department.

"I hated woodworking in school," Joel admitted. "It wasn't until I started working at the plantation, using hand tools and trying to decipher how things were made, that it became actually interesting for me. The historical aspect of it was what fascinated me. If it were just doing straight carpentry, I probably wouldn't have stayed with it."

How to Get Started. Joel advised taking a few courses in historic trades or historic preservation. "But," he cautioned, "the skills we need are particular to Plimoth Plantation. Outside courses would be painted with such a broad brush, but what's done at Plimoth Plantation is very focused on a particular group of people in a very short time span.

"The best qualification would be a lot of hand-tool work. The tools haven't changed that much over the centuries. Try taking a tree and make a table or a chair from it. That's the best way to learn the art."

Because of limited budgets and a low turnover, openings are rare. However, there is an occasional internship as well as a volunteer program that could help you get your foot in the door.

What It's Like to Be a Potter at Plimoth Plantation

Four potters in the Crafts Center at Plimoth Plantation demonstrate seventeenth-century throwing techniques, though only one potter is on duty at a time. They also make all the pieces that are used in the village by the interpreters. During the winter months when the museum is closed to visitors, the potters make enough items to replenish the stock.

Deb Mason spends several hours a week in the Crafts Center and is the supervisor of the other potters. She also has her own home studio, where she teaches pottery classes, does commission work, and makes pieces for display at various galleries. Deb talked about her job:

"In the Crafts Center, we don't claim to be seventeenth-century people because pottery wasn't done in the village in 1627. But because of this, we have an advantage. We can talk to visitors in a way that's totally different from the interpreters. A visitor might go to the village, then come back to the Crafts Center to ask a question that the seventeenth-century interpreters couldn't answer. The interpreters have to speak as though they are Pilgrims. They wouldn't have any knowledge beyond 1627.

"For now we are working with twentieth-century equipment, though we are discussing the possibility of going back in time, using a kick wheel and a wood-burning stove. The electric wheels we use now might make throwing look faster and easier than it was in the seventeenth century, but the techniques are still very much the same.

"The difference is we have to make only period pieces, and there some of the difficulties come in. For example, we're trying to find the right clay bodies to work with. We have a few original pieces on display to study, and you can see the clay color and texture. We've been experimenting, trying to develop clay bodies that are close to the original.

"That's been fairly successful, but we're having a tough time with glazes. They used a lot of lead back then. In fact, most every glaze was lead-based. Because we sell the pieces we make in the gift shop and they're also used in the village every day, we've been trying to get away from lead. It's hard to come up with glazes that have the same shine and the same colors; lead has a very typical look. We're using a ground glass that melts at a low temperature, which is a characteristic of lead, and produces similar results.

"We make ointment pots that held salves and other healing lotions, apothecary jars, bowls, porringers for porridge, oil lamps, candlesticks, and pipkins—little cooking pots with a side handle and three legs on the bottom.

"We also make a lot of three-handled cups. Pilgrims usually shared their eating implements. The cups are funny-looking things—a popular item in the craft shop.

"Back then the pottery was hastily thrown. There's a real earthy quality to the pieces. Their perceptions of what was beautiful and what was utilitarian were different. What they strove for was extremely rough by today's standards.

"My biggest problem is remembering not to throw too well. The advantage to that, though, for potters wanting to work here, is that a high degree of skill is not necessary."

Background. Deb earned her bachelor's degree in art with a major in ceramics in 1973 from Bennington College in Vermont. She taught ceramics full-time for thirteen years at a private school and was the head of the art department her last few years there. She joined the staff at Plimoth Plantation in 1992.

Salaries. Salaries for craft workers differ depending on whether they are full-time or part-time. Part-timers are paid hourly.

....

Researcher

Researchers form the backbone behind every living history museum. Without their efforts, the ability to re-create authentic period characters, to accurately restore historic buildings, or to reproduce a facsimile of daily life would be an impossible task.

What It's Like to Be a Researcher at Plimoth Plantation

Carolyn Travers, director of research at Plimoth Plantation, talked about her job:

"We have four sites at Plimoth Plantation: the 1627 English Village; the *Mayflower II*; the Wampanoag Homesite; and the Carriage House Crafts Center. We research anything we need for our program, from what was the period attitude toward toads and how a character felt about being her husband's third wife to the correct way to cook a particular dish or some obscure point of Calvinist theology.

"The women are more difficult to research than the men because there is less documented information on them. You are forced into re-creating a more typical persona than the actual character, sort of a generic portrayal. In general, we research the life and genealogical background and social history for all the characters we portray.

"In our research, we use a variety of sources—court records and genealogical research done by professional genealogists, such as the General Society of *Mayflower* Descendants, or writers for the *American Genealogist* or other genealogy periodicals.

"We also have researchers in other departments. For example, the authenticity of buildings and structures is done more by our curatorial department."

Background. Carolyn attended Earlham College, a small Quaker school in Richmond, Indiana, where she earned a bachelor's degree in fine arts with a concentration in history. She went on to Simmons Graduate School of Library and Information Science in Boston and earned a master's degree in 1981 in library and information science with a concentration in research methods.

Carolyn grew up in Plymouth and started work at the age of fourteen as a part-time Pilgrim. After she finished her master's degree, she returned to Plimoth Plantation as a researcher.

Qualifications. Carolyn pointed out that researching is a competitive field, and that a higher degree, in history or library science with a research methods concentration, is necessary. A candidate is not expected to have a general body of knowledge about the specific time period, but he or she must have strong research skills, talent, and experience.

Salaries. New graduates might begin with yearly salaries in the high teens or low twenties. "You don't do it for the money," Carolyn stressed. "There are a lot of psychological payments. One of the satisfactions is to be able to change someone's mind about the stereotypes surrounding early colonists."

Researchers can find work in a variety of other settings as well: university archaeology and history departments, preservation boards, libraries and archives, government offices, and history museums.

Other Jobs at Living History Museums

Following is a list of other job areas that can be found in various living history museums. Many are also discussed in detail in later chapters.

- Archaeology
- Architecture
- Building and grounds maintenance
- Business affairs
- Collections management
- Curatorship
- Development and Membership
- Educational Programs
- Information
- Personnel
- Public Relations
- Sales
- Security
- Visitor Services

The National Park Service

Interpreting Our National Treasures

···

A bureau within the U.S. Department of the Interior, the National Park Service employs more than 20,000 paid employees and more than 140,000 volunteers in managing the federal natural and recreational areas across the country, including the Grand Canyon, Yellowstone National Park, and Lake Mead. In addition, more than two hundred sites of cultural and historic significance fall under the Park Service's jurisdiction and provide numerous employment opportunities of interest to history buffs.

In general, most of the history-related jobs are located in the mid-Atlantic, Southeast, and national capital regions; most archaeology- and geology-related positions are in the West and Southwest. The various sites encompass battlefields, national monuments, historical and military parks, forts, memorials, and landmark formations.

Because most sites are not located near major cities, serious candidates must, for the most part, be prepared to relocate. Housing may or may not be provided, depending upon the site and your position.

The National Park Service Website

On the Internet, visit the National Park Service's website at www.nps.gov, where you will find a link to job and volunteer opportunities. You'll also find general information on National Park Service careers and application processes. There are convenient links to the Office of Personnel Management and to the volunteers program.

The website also includes a guide to volunteer and archaeological fieldwork opportunities both in and out of the National Park Service, with information on special archaeological weeks in specific states. Visit www.cr.nps.gov/museum to learn about the National Park Service's Museum Management Program, including events, exhibits, and opportunities.

Park Ranger (Interpretation)

The National Park Service hires three categories of park rangers, usually on a seasonal basis: enforcement, general, and interpretation. Most history buffs apply for positions in the interpretation category.

Duties vary greatly from position to position and site to site, but rangers in the interpretation division are usually responsible for developing and presenting programs that explain a park's historic, cultural, or archaeological features. This is done through talks, demonstrations, and guided walking tours.

Rangers also sit at information desks, provide visitor services, or participate in conservation or restoration projects. Entry-level employees may also collect fees, provide first aid, and operate audiovisual equipment.

Career Potential

Park rangers begin their service at various grades, depending upon their experience and qualifications. From the point of job entry, rangers may move through the ranks to become district rangers, park managers, and staff specialists in interpretation, resource management, park planning, and related areas.

Rangers' responsibilities and independence increase as their influence covers more staff and area. Upper-level managers in the Park Service are recruited primarily for their managerial capabilities. Keen competition exists for park ranger positions at all grade levels.

As of 2008, examples of summer jobs and hourly wages for park rangers were as follows:

Fire Lookout (Park Ranger), Colorado	$13.83
Park Ranger (Law enforcement–Protection), Pennsylvania	$17.64
Park Ranger (Interpretation), Washington State, San Juan Island	$14.24

Education and Earnings

When it comes to determining a candidate's eligibility for employment, and at which salary level, the National Park Service weighs several factors. Those with the least experience or education will begin at the lowest federal government salary grade of GS-2. The requirements for that grade level are only six months of experience in related work or a high school diploma or its equivalent.

The more relevant work experience or education an employee has, the higher the salary level. For example, level GS-4 requires eighteen months of general experience in park operations or in related fields and six months of specialized experience—or one ninety-day season as a Seasonal Park Ranger at the GS-3 level. Completion of two full academic years of college may be substituted for experience if the course work covers social science, history, archaeology, parks and recreation management, or other related disciplines.

Close-Up: St. Augustine—America's Oldest City

Viewing the city from an aerial vantage point or entering from the south across the Bridge of Lions (named for the Spanish explorer Ponce de León), St. Augustine, Florida, America's oldest city, resembles a European burg, or a medieval hamlet. Fairy-tale castles with spires and turrets rise above roofs of gingerbread-trimmed dollhouses. Horse-drawn carriages, stone walls, city gates, and a fort constructed from blocks of coquina, a native shell-based stone quarried across the bay on Anastasia Island, add to the fanciful effect.

St. George Street, said to be one of the oldest roadways in the oldest city in the country, was fully restored in the mid-1970s. On either side of the narrow promenade, painted signs adorning vintage buildings proclaim "Oldest Wooden Schoolhouse," built during the first Spanish occupation before the American Revolution, and "Oldest Store," a museum with a collection of more than one hundred thousand of yesterday's mementos.

St. Augustine's oldest house is one of the most-studied and best-documented houses in the United States. It was originally built with palm thatchings covering a crude structure of logs and boards, then restored after a fire in 1702 with coquina walls and flooring made from a mixture of lime, shell, and sand. The house provides a record of life in St. Augustine for more than four hundred years. Archaeologists, through digs and research, have verified continuous occupancy of that particular site dating from the early 1600s to the present day—in spite of raids, looting, and fire.

Nearby, the St. Augustine Old Jail, listed in the National Register of Historic Places, contains original weapons used in long-ago crimes and offers an interesting courtyard display of historical artifacts. The building, with living quarters for the sheriff and his family, served the county until 1953.

South of the old city gate is St. Augustine's Colonial Spanish Quarter. In this living history museum are restored homes and gardens more than 250 years old. Guides and artisans dressed in period clothing re-create the daily lifestyle, giving visitors an inside look at life as it was for eighteenth-century soldiers and settlers.

Castillo de San Marcos National Monument, built by the Spanish between 1672 and 1695 and now run by the National Park Service, is the oldest fort in the United States.

After Ponce de León claimed Florida, it took more than fifty years for Spain to establish a permanent settlement in St. Augustine. The early Spaniards had many clashes with colonialists in neighboring Georgia and North and South Carolina. St. Augustine was twice burned to the ground. The fort was finally constructed to secure the city.

Lacking brick-making materials, the Spanish used blocks of coquina. Softer than brick, it helped the fort withstand numerous attacks, its walls absorbing the impact of iron cannonballs rather than shattering, as brick would have.

Unfortunately, though, the coquina tends to break off when touched, and portions of the fort have been eroding away. The damage is irreparable; a mortar substitute can be used to patch up the surface here and there, but the park rangers warn visitors not to lean against the walls.

The fort raised different flags above its walls many times during the years, through wartime and peace, through treaties, trades, and negotiations, but in 1821 it changed hands for the last time when the United States acquired Florida from Spain.

The fort is also significant in that it houses what are claimed to be the nation's oldest toilets.

Further Reading

America's First City: St. Augustine's Historic Neighborhoods, by Karen Harvey, illustrated by Nina McGuire (Lake Buena Vista, FL: Tailored Tours Publications, 1997).

What It's Like to Be a Park Ranger at Castillo de San Marcos

Gordie Wilson graduated from college in 1977 with a degree in parks and recreation and immediately began working for the National Park Service. Twenty-five years later, in addition to his post as superintendent of Castillo de San Marcos National Monument, he was also in charge of nearby Fort Matanzas National Monument. Gordie talked about the duties of a park ranger:

"There really is no such thing as a typical day. Duties are varied, and there is always the unexpected. A park ranger might begin the day sitting at the ticket booth collecting fees, then go inside the fort to give a two-hour presentation to visitors, explaining the fort's history. Later, costumed park rangers set off the cannons in a daily display, while others ensure that would-be treasure hunters are not defacing the property with shovels and metal detectors.

"If a visitor has a heart attack, which is not a rare occurrence, then trained park rangers will administer CPR or other forms of first aid. A park ranger must be prepared to take on a variety of duties."

Getting Your Foot in the Door

"Competition for jobs, especially at the most well-known sites, can be fierce," Gordie explained, "but the National Park Service employs a huge permanent staff, and this is supplemented tenfold by an essential seasonal workforce during peak visitation periods.

"The best way for a newcomer to break in is to start off with seasonal employment during school breaks. With a couple of summer seasons under your belt, the doors will open more easily for permanent employment."

And, because of Office of Personnel Management regulations, veterans of the U.S. Armed Forces have a decided advantage. Depending upon their experience, they may be given preference over other applicants.

Summer Employment Opportunities

The Historic American Buildings Survey/Historic American Engineering Record (HABS/HAER), a division of the National Park Service, seeks applications from qualified individuals for summer employment in documenting historic sites and structures of architectural, landscape, and technological significance throughout the country. Duties involve on-site fieldwork and preparation of measured and interpretive drawings and written historical reports for the HABS/HAER Collection at the Prints and Photographs Division of the Library of Congress. Projects last twelve weeks, beginning in May and June.

Visit the website at www.nps.gov/history/hdp/jobs/summer .htm for forms and more detailed information on how to apply.

Applying for Temporary Employment

Annual recruitment for the next summer's employment usually begins September 1, with a January 15 deadline. Some sites, such as Death Valley or Everglades National Park, also have a busy winter season. The winter recruitment period is June 1 through July 15. Other factors are as follows:

1. Applicants may apply for employment year-round.
2. Positions covered under this system include:
   a. Park Ranger (Interpretation) GS-5 and GS-7
   b. Park Ranger (General) GS-5 and GS-7
   c. Park Ranger (Law Enforcement) GS-5 and GS-7
   d. Park Guide GS-4, GS-5, and GS-6
   e. Visitor Use Assistant GS-4, GS-5, and GS-6
   f. Biological Technician GS-4, GS-5, GS-6, and GS-7
3. All applications must be postmarked before the closing date.
4. Applicants may apply for any and all park opportunities.
5. Applicants may update their applications at any time, day or night, as long as it is before the closing date of the announcement.

6. Applicants only have to answer the Core Questions section of the application once.
7. Applicants must answer the Specialty Questions for each position for which they are applying.
8. Go to www.nps.gov/personnel to learn more about job categories with the National Park Service. Visit www.usajobs.gov to search active job listings, create a resume, and apply online.

You can also contact one of the regional offices of the National Park Service for local information. Addresses for each of these offices are provided in Appendix C.

....

Historian

In addition to park ranger positions, the National Park Service has another category called, simply, Historian. Duties involve conducting research and producing inventories and reports on specific sites, structures, and technical processes.

Historians also work with the National Register of Historic Places, a branch of the Interagency Resources Division that is also administered by the National Park Service.

....

Close-Up: National Register of Historic Places

The National Register of Historic Places is the United States' official list of national resources worthy of preservation. Part of a national program, the National Register of Historic Places supports public and private efforts to identify, evaluate, and protect America's historic and archaeological resources.

The National Register includes all historic areas in the National Park System, National Historic Landmarks designated by the Secretary of the Interior, and properties such as historic districts, sites, buildings, structures, and objects significant in American history, architecture, archaeology, engineering, and culture.

Each year more than two thousand nominations are put forward; the vast majority meet all eligibility requirements and are consequently entered in the National Register. The following list provides a few interesting entries.

- **Moulin Rouge Hotel**, Las Vegas, Nevada. Of exceptional importance in the history of integration, this was the first Las Vegas club built (1955) especially to cater to a racially integrated audience.
- **Ma Rainey House**, Columbus, Georgia. This was home to Gertrude Pridgett, also known as "Ma" Rainey, who was dubbed Mother of the Blues for her contribution to the world of music.
- **Luber School**, Stone County in the Arkansas Ozarks. This one-room stone building is remarkable as a monument to educational reforms both in Arkansas and nationally.
- **"Galloping Gertie,"** Puget Sound, Washington. The ruins of a collapsed suspension bridge lie submerged in Puget Sound near Tacoma, Washington. The bridge's failure ushered in new developments in bridge design and aerodynamics.
- **Eric Ellis Soderholtz Cottage**, West Gouldsboro, Maine. Home to the noted potter and photographer, the cottage was built by the artist and is one of the state's most distinctive arts and crafts cottages and an important example of craftsman architecture in rural America.

Admission to the National Register of Historic Places brings national recognition, various tax benefits, and the potential for federal grants for historic preservation when funds are available. Nominations are usually begun on the local and state level, by individuals and agencies, and then are submitted to the National Register of Historic Places for final review.

What It's Like to Be a Historian with the National Register

The National Register of Historic Places employs a number of full-time professional historians, architectural historians, and archaeologists. Historian Antoinette Lee had been with the National Register since November of 1989 and discussed her job:

"I coordinate our National Register program. We produce a lot of technical information on evaluating properties for the National Register. I handle public accessibility by promoting the National Register's Starter Kit through advertisements. The kit is helpful to people considering nominating a property. I also issue press releases on new monthly listings.

"All the historians are assigned different regions in the country; I am responsible for the register's programs in the western states. I evaluate the nominations to the register that come in, then admit them if they're eligible.

"We participate in different workshops and seminars and get out in the field occasionally to meet people on the front line of historic preservation at the state and local levels."

Background. Antoinette's interest in history was largely influenced by her grandmother, who, in the 1920s and 1930s, worked toward the preservation of Pullman, Illinois—George Pullman's socially progressive and comprehensively planned community for railway employees and their families.

At the time of her interview, Antoinette had more than twenty years of experience in the field. She earned a bachelor's degree in history at the University of Pennsylvania and her doctorate in American civilization from the George Washington University in Washington, D.C.

During the bicentennial era in the 1970s, she did freelance research work for various historians, architectural historians, and preservationists who were involved in major studies commemorating the 1976 bicentennial. One of her projects was a history of state capitol buildings. In the late 1970s and early 1980s, she worked as education coordinator for the National Trust for Historic Preservation, which is a private, nonprofit preservation organization. After that, she worked for eight years as a private consultant in historic preservation. When a friend showed her the announcement for the position of historian with the National Register of Historic Places, Antoinette applied and was selected.

What It Takes to Be a Historian

A candidate for the job of historian should be willing to serve the public and have an understanding of history at national, state, and local levels. It is also important to be aware of historic preservation needs and to be able to help people in achieving their goals.

To qualify as a historian, which merits a federal government rating of GS-5 through GS-15, applicants must have at least a bachelor's degree in architectural history, history of technology, American civilization, historic preservation, or a related field. A graduate degree is preferred. Having several years of field experience is also important in order to be able to adequately evaluate nominated properties.

For current salary information in each of these grades, check with the U.S. Office of Personnel Management, present in most major cities, or with any federal government agency.

Getting a Foot in the Door

Paid internships are available through the National Council for Preservation Education, but the number offered is relatively small. There are generally numerous job and internship opportunities at the state and local levels. You can start your investigations at your local library. For more information call or write:

National Register of Historic Places
National Park Service
1201 Eye Street NW, Eighth Floor
Washington, DC 20005
www.cr.nps.gov/nr

CHAPTER FOUR

History Museums

Displaying the Past

Nothing makes history come more alive than to hold a piece of it in your hands. From acquiring collections and preserving them to explaining and displaying them, history buffs in history museums have the chance to work with every aspect of the relics and other forms of physical evidence of the past.

There are thousands of history museums across the country. They are housed in intentionally designed and built structures or in historic buildings and homes that are open to the public. Many are large enterprises employing scores of professionals to handle day-to-day operations. Other museums are small and operate with only a handful of employees and dedicated volunteers.

The larger the museum, the more specialized an employee's duties are. Professionals in midsize or small museums must be willing to take on a variety of tasks. However, knowledge of or familiarity with all areas of museum functions, in addition to a strong background in a particular discipline, are important qualifications for any staff member.

Along with the proper educational achievements, the American Association of Museums (AAM) suggests these additional qualifications for museum personnel:

- A museum professional should have a familiarity with the history, goals, and functions of museums; a knowledge of and commitment to the AAM statement on ethics; and a willingness to improve skills by study and by attendance at training sessions, seminars, and professional conferences.

- Dedication, integrity, diplomacy, and a commitment to thoroughness and accuracy are demanded of all museum professionals. The ability to communicate orally and in writing and to work constructively with associates is essential.
- An awareness of legal issues affecting museums and the ability to prepare and interpret budgets and grant applications are required of all positions. Additional knowledge, skills, and abilities, such as a second language, typing, and word processing, and familiarity with the museum's community and its resources may be required for certain positions and are always beneficial and desirable.

The AAM has identified dozens of direct and museum-related career categories. Several of interest to history lovers are examined here, along with the expected requirements for levels of education, experience, knowledge, abilities, and skills.

Collections Manager

The collections manager supervises, numbers, catalogs, and stores the specimens within each division of the museum.

- **Education requirements.** An undergraduate degree in the area of the museum's specialization is the minimum requirement. An advanced degree in museum studies with a concentration in a specific discipline is recommended.
- **Experience.** Most museums prefer candidates to have at least three years of experience in a museum registration department or a position in which the main duties are the technical aspects of handling, storage, preservation, and cataloging.

- **Knowledge and skills.** Collections managers need to know information management techniques, be able to accurately identify objects within the museum's collection, and know security practices and environmental controls.

Curator

Curators are specialists in a particular academic discipline relevant to a museum's collections. They are generally responsible for the care and interpretation of all objects and specimens on loan or belonging to the museum, and they are fully knowledgeable about each object's history and importance.

Depending upon the museum and its areas of interest, curators can work with textiles and costumes, paintings, memorabilia, historic structures, crafts, furniture, coins, or a variety of other historically significant items.

- **Education requirements.** A curator usually holds an advanced degree with a concentration in an area related to the museum's collections.
- **Experience.** Three years of experience in a museum or related educational or research facility would usually be required before a candidate could advance to a full curatorial position.
- **Knowledge and skills.** The curator must have the ability to explain and interpret the collection to the public and be familiar with the techniques of selection, evaluation, preservation, restoration, and exhibition of the museum's collection.

Director

A museum director is responsible for acquisitions, preservation, research, and presentation. The director is also involved with making policies, handling funding and budgets, supervising staff, and coordinating museum activities.

- **Education requirements.** An advanced degree in the area of the museum's specialty is required, with specific course work in museum administration.
- **Experience.** A museum director needs three years or more of management experience in a museum or related institution.
- **Knowledge and skills.** A director should have specialized knowledge of at least one area of the museum's collections or in the management of the particular type of museum. His or her area of expertise must also include implementing policies and financial planning.

Educator

An educator's main function is to enhance public awareness of and access to the museum's collections. To do this, an educator designs and implements programs encompassing a variety of media and techniques and arranges for special events, workshops, and teacher training programs. In addition, an educator might train docents and tour guides and might have other supervisory and administrative duties.

- **Education requirements.** The job requires an advanced degree in education, museum education, or one of the museum's specialty areas.
- **Experience.** Two years of experience in a museum education department or other related facility are needed.
- **Knowledge and skills.** An educator needs the ability to prepare material for publications and exhibitions, skills in oral and written communication, and knowledge of school systems' curricula and research techniques.

Exhibit Designer

Exhibit designers work closely with curatorial and educational personnel to convey ideas through permanent or temporary exhibits. They use drawings, scale models, special lighting, and other techniques. An exhibit designer can have administrative responsibilities and may supervise the production of exhibits.

- **Education requirements.** A degree or certification in graphic or industrial design, commercial art or communications arts, architecture, interior design, or studio arts is needed.
- **Experience.** Designers need to gain experience in exhibition design and related construction work with wood, metal, or plastics. A portfolio of past and current work is necessary.
- **Knowledge and skills.** Skills in conceptualizing exhibit designs, creating mechanical drawings, making refined aesthetic judgments, and supervising exhibit installation are essential.

Salaries

Earnings of curators and other museum professionals vary considerably by type and size of employer and often by specialty. Average salaries in the federal government, for example, are usually higher than those in religious organizations. Salaries of curators in large, well-funded museums can be several times higher than those in small ones.

- **Archivists.** As of May 2006, according to data reported in the *Occupational Outlook Handbook*, median annual earnings of archivists were approximately $40,730. The middle 50 percent earned between $30,610 and $53,990.

The lowest 10 percent earned less than $23,890, and the highest 10 percent earned more than $73,060.

- **Curators.** Median annual earnings were $46,300, with the lowest 10 percent earning less than $26,320 and the highest earning more than $80,030.
- **Museum technicians and conservators.** These professionals earned a median annual income of $34,340, with the lowest 10 percent earning less than $20,600 and the highest 10 percent earning more than $61,270.

Close-Up: The Smithsonian Institution

When most Americans think about spending a day at the mall, they've got "shopping till they drop" on their minds. But residents and seasoned visitors in Washington, D.C., know that the Mall, located between the U.S. Capitol and the Washington Monument, is a nicely manicured strip of land that houses several museums of the Smithsonian Institution, the world's largest museum complex. The Smithsonian is composed of nineteen museums and galleries—two are located in New York—as well as the National Zoo. The museums are named here:

- Anacostia Community Museum
- Arthur M. Sackler Gallery
- Arts and Industries Building
- Cooper-Hewitt, National Design Museum (New York)
- Freer Gallery of Art
- Hirshhorn Museum and Sculpture Garden
- National Air and Space Museum
- National Museum of African Art
- National Museum of American History
- National Museum of Natural History
- National Museum of the American Indian (also in New York and Maryland)
- National Portrait Gallery

- National Postal Museum
- Renwick Gallery
- Smithsonian American Art Museum
- Smithsonian Information Center (the Castle)

The Castle houses the Smithsonian's central administration offices. Each individual museum has its own director and staff. The chief executive officer of the Smithsonian is given the title of secretary. The institution is governed by a board of regents that, by law, is composed of the vice president of the United States, the chief justice of the United States, three members of the Senate, three members of the House of Representatives, and nine private citizens. Traditionally, the chief justice of the United States has served as chancellor of the museum.

The National Museum of American History, which is part of the Smithsonian Institution complex on the National Mall, is devoted to the exhibition, care, and study of artifacts that reflect the experience of the American people. The museum receives more than five million visitors a year. It has the responsibility for preserving the more than sixteen million objects it has acquired during the last century, and it has more than 460 employees on staff.

What It's Like to Be a Curator at the Museum of American History

When Charles McGovern became supervisor of the American History museum's Division of Community Life, he oversaw a group of technicians, specialists, collection-based researchers, curators, and support staff. He was also a curator, responsible for the museum's collections of twentieth-century consumerism and popular culture. This department covers the history of entertainment, leisure, recreation, and commerce.

The exhibits within this department are possibly the most popular and the most well-known of all. Visitors to the museum come to view Judy Garland's ruby slippers from *The Wizard of Oz*;

Carroll O'Connor's well-worn chair used by his character, Archie Bunker, in "All in the Family"; and ventriloquist Edgar Bergen's famous wooden dummy, Charlie McCarthy.

Charles McGovern's interest in cultural history began at an early age. He watched a lot of television, listened to the radio, and participated in the mass popular culture in the 1960s. His father and mother told him about the times when they were growing up, sharing with him stories about the early days of radio. When Charles got to high school and read books his teachers recommended, he realized that Babe Ruth and Laurel and Hardy and the Marx brothers, personalities he cared very deeply about, were as much a part of history as Calvin Coolidge or the First World War. Charles talked about his job:

"Part of my profession as a historian is to be a decoder or an explainer, to go back into the heads and the lives and the beliefs of our ancestors. And here, we try to do that respectfully, understanding the world as they saw it. As we do that, we see how culture reflects the times—the fears and ideals and problems of a given society. You cannot look at certain creations of our popular culture without seeing those kinds of elements in them.

"As a curator, I am responsible for the creation and maintenance of the collections in my subject area. I document the history of the everyday life of American people. The major outline for my job puts me in charge of building collections, developing exhibitions, conducting research, writing, public service, public speaking, and being a graduate advisor to eleven research fellows.

"Specifically, my job is divided into three parts: acquisitions, which means acquiring new objects and exhibits for the museum; exhibiting and interpreting; and research.

"The collections I am responsible for include a lot of the things related to the history of American entertainment: a hat that Jimmy Durante used in his stage appearances; Ann Miller's tap shoes; Howdy Doody; Mr. Moose, Bunny Rabbit, and Grandfather Clock from Captain Kangaroo; the suit of armor worn by Francis

X. Bushman in the original 1925 movie *Ben-Hur*; Carol Burnett's char lady costume; Mister Rogers's sweater; Harrison Ford's Indiana Jones outfit (his leather jacket and hat); Tom Selleck's ring from 'Magnum, P.I.' and his Hawaiian shirt and baseball cap; old 78 rpm records; movie posters; and comic books. We also look for collections that give us insight into American consumerism and commerce. We have the bonnet that was worn by the woman who posed for the Sun-Maid raisin box; a huge collection of turn-of-the-century advertising, marketing, and packaging items from the Hills Bros. Coffee Company; and a collection of memorabilia from world's fairs from 1851 to 1988.

"To build our collections, we depend largely on people donating items. In fact, almost everything has been donated. We have very little money in our acquisitions budget. We can't compete in a very inflated market with the galleries and people who deal with 'collectibles.' People must be willing to donate, so we look for people who either don't need the money or get the point of what we're trying to do.

"Sometimes we're not able to accept everything that is being offered. Someone called once and wanted to donate Charlie Chaplin's cane. But first, how do I know it was his cane? It's impossible to document that. And second, Chaplin probably went through thousands of canes. Those bamboo things snapped very easily. Something like that we couldn't take.

"And although I must be familiar with every piece's history, the range and variety of items I am responsible for is staggering. It's not as if I were a curator of painting, where I'm trained in oils and brush techniques. Once in a while I have to confer with an appraiser or dealer to determine authenticity.

"Once a donation has been accepted, we can never promise that it will go on display. Less than 2 percent of our collection is on display at any given time; the rest is kept in storage. Although some exhibits, such as the ruby slippers or Archie's chair, are permanent, others rotate.

"Part of my job is to decide what gets exhibited, what gets stored, what is rotated. And to care for all the items, to make sure they don't deteriorate, we need to remove even permanent exhibits from time to time. People travel a long way expecting to see a certain item, and if it's not on display they're usually upset. They don't realize they should check with us first if they're coming to see something in particular. We took Charlie McCarthy off to clean him one day, and within a half an hour we had three phone calls asking, 'Where is Charlie McCarthy?'

"The exhibiting side of my job is really a team effort. Exhibit designers work with curators to decide how an item should be displayed. The designer is responsible for the layout of objects and text and graphics and props. A conservator, someone who takes care of the actual repair or maintenance of an object, would be responsible for the 'prescription'—'This piece needs to be lit with not more than thirty foot-candles,' for example.

"But I feel that research is really my first duty. All the collecting and exhibiting doesn't mean anything unless you have something to say. You have to figure out first what point you're making. Our point is the showing of everyday life of the American people, and for earlier times that's something that has to be researched. Of course, you do research to support the things you already have in your collection, but the research also helps you to determine what you should be out there collecting."

Background. Charles studied at Swarthmore College in Pennsylvania and finished in 1980 with a bachelor's degree, with honors, in history. He immediately began graduate school at Harvard and earned his master's degree in history in 1983 and his doctorate in American civilization in 1993. During that time, Charles taught history at Harvard, and then from 1986 through 1987 he served at the Smithsonian as a research fellow. In 1988 he became a full-time curator.

The Smithsonian as Training Ground. Every year, the Smithsonian awards dozens of research fellowships, providing funding to doctoral candidates and access to museum collections. To be hired as a curator, candidates must have a doctorate or be almost finished with it. Entry-level positions include technicians and specialists and research-related jobs. Paid internships and volunteer positions are usually available and a good way to get a foot in the door.

As Charles pointed out, jobs for curators at the Smithsonian seldom become available. But because the Smithsonian has a certain reputation and skill in training, it's a good place to gain a foundation and then go out to other areas or institutions for work later on. An internship at the Smithsonian will go a long way in securing employment elsewhere.

Salaries. A beginning curator who has almost completed a doctorate might come in at entry level somewhere in the mid-$30,000s. The next jump would be to the low $40,000s. Staff members at the Smithsonian are employees of the federal government and follow the GS scale.

What It's Like to Be an Exhibit Designer at the Museum of American History

Many small and even midsize institutions do not have room in their budgets for a specialist exhibit designer. In a situation such as that, one or two people, the director or the curator, might perform the functions of an exhibit designer in addition to the duties of their own specialties. Or, in some cases, the museum will contract with an outside firm for exhibit design work.

The Smithsonian Institution, a large operation, employs more than twenty exhibit designers and assistants, and several of the designers work specifically for the National Museum of American History.

Hank Grasso was a senior exhibit designer working in all of the different departments within the National Museum of American History. Hank came to the Smithsonian in 1990 as a visual information specialist, the government's job title for an exhibit designer. He usually functioned as part of a team of professionals including curators, collections managers, conservators, scriptwriters, audience advocates—or educators, as they are most often known—and project managers. He came on board specifically to work with the American Encounters Show, the museum's Columbus five-hundredth-year presentation.

Hank also worked on the designs for the "Working People of Philadelphia" in the Life in America exhibit, Science in American Life, the East Broad Top Railroad, Manufactured Weather, and Feed Bags as Fashion, a popular exhibit on an unusual fashion trend. Hank discussed the process of exhibit design:

"If you have a thousand images and ten square feet of space, you need to come up with a vehicle that will allow those images to be displayed. For example, you can compress them into a video disk or a series of slide presentations or storyboards. We look at the information we're wanting to convey and then translate it visually, keeping an eye to spatial allocations.

"There are two distinct models you can follow. With the traditional model, the cast of characters involved stay in very rigid roles: the curator passes abstract ideas to the designer, who then translates them into a physical presentation. The curator is responsible for content, ideas, and the written word; the designer is responsible for the environment, aesthetics, and graphic design.

"A more modern approach is called a collaborative exhibition development, involving a team of professionals working together. We worked this way when we were creating the American Encounters show, a permanent exhibit at the Smithsonian. We created design tools so all parts of the team could understand each other. We could look over each other's shoulders and know what we were seeing."

Putting an Exhibit Together. These are just a few of the many steps a collaborative team follows when working on a new exhibit:

1. Listen to ideas and identify interpretive goals. Why are we telling this story? What is the most important message we want to convey?
2. Look at the available space and create a floor plan.
3. Combine steps 1 and 2 by prioritizing ideas and looking at the elements that will hold the exhibit together.
4. Decide how it will be done—presentation vehicles, techniques, and technology.
5. Choose the objects and images that will best tell the story.
6. Make a scale model that renders all the individual objects, labels, and graphic images.
7. Translate the scale model into design control drawings, sets of drawings that have to do with the general contracting and building of spaces and with the making of exhibit parts.
8. Write the script and labels for the exhibit.
9. Begin the competitive bid process for general contracting.
10. Construct a full-scale model.
11. Conduct audience research. How does the audience react? Does the audience understand the materials and ideas being presented?
12. Do final construction.
13. Handle promotional and outreach elements.

Background. Hank attended Denison University, a small liberal arts school in Ohio, from 1972 to 1974. During his two years there, he had a chance to get a good overview of the various courses and decide what he wanted to pursue. He then transferred to Penn State and studied in the wood products division, specializing in wood as an art medium, looking at both its aesthetic and structural uses. He also combined his study of wood products with courses in the architecture department, including drafting and drawing, and graduated in 1976 with a bachelor's degree in interdisciplinary studies. He later went back to school at Pratt Institute in New York and took graduate courses to increase his conceptualization skills and learn more about different fabricating techniques.

Between his time at Penn State and Pratt, Hank worked for a couple of different private design firms that were contracted by various museums. While building up his portfolio, he had an opportunity to work on exhibit designs for the John F. Kennedy Library in Boston, the Basketball Hall of Fame, the Bowling Hall of Fame, the New York Historical Society, the United Nations, the Metropolitan Museum of Art, the Frederick Douglas National Historic Site, and the Buffalo Bill Historical Center.

In 1996, Hank started his own firm, Planning and Design, Inc., in Kensington, Maryland, doing contract work for the Smithsonian Institution as well as for other clients.

Getting on the Right Path. Today there are three main educational preparation choices for someone wishing to pursue a career as an exhibit designer.

1. Institutions such as Pratt or Parsons School of Design offer good courses in industrial, graphic, and commercial design.
2. Some universities can provide a liberal arts education combined with certain skill courses.
3. Professional programs in a field such as architecture provide appropriate training.

Hank suggested that once your theoretical education is completed, so much more of what is still out there to study can be learned through internships and working for diverse design firms, which also gives the new exhibit designer a chance to build a portfolio, an important tool for moving on to the next position.

Salaries. Exhibit designers work as employees in museums or for private firms that contract with museums. Not surprisingly, salaries paid by the private companies often top those that many museums can pay, even if the designer is doing the same work in the same institution. Annual salaries for entry-level workers in museums can range from $18,000 to $27,000 and are several thousand dollars higher in a private firm. An exhibit designer with more than ten years of experience could expect to earn somewhere in the $40,000s to $60,000s.

Notes from a Student Intern's Journal. In addition to his other duties, Hank was often responsible for the supervision of interns. Kendra Lambert, from Auburn University in Alabama, was one of his students. She spent her last summer in college learning about graphic design at the National Museum of American History. Here are some of the notes she kept on her experiences there:

"Attended staff meetings for American Encounters. Met curators, designers, educators, and the team writer along with other interns working on the project. At these meetings, each team member's thoughts were expressed concerning deadlines, progress to date, and objectives. Interaction is clearly important to working as a team.

"I helped build a prototype of two cases, Pueblo and Spanish missions, within the exhibit. Maps were enlarged from photocopies and mounted on foam core. Time lines were set on the Macintosh using a PageMaker program, then cut and mounted to be used on a larger scale. The purpose of the prototype was to test audience reaction to typefaces used. Hank wanted to find out if people are sensitive to these subtleties in type and if symbols help some people break down information. Curators also reworded some of the labels. It meant more work for the design department, but it was important to have an accurate representation of the cases.

"I learned to draw objects to scale working on the Feed Bags as Fashion case. I was responsible for the title logo. Hank wanted to work from the original stencil face from an actual feed bag. It became too complex to create letterforms when we had no reference.

"During Feed Bags, I got to work in the Exhibit Production Lab. I helped set type for labels, I observed the process for silk screening, I positioned the text on panels. It was great to be part of production! And within hours of opening the exhibit, the press was there. It was great—and such a huge audience response. People loved it.

"I have learned that designing exhibits requires a person who is flexible to schedule the meetings that are a part of working in a team and still complete the required drawing and model work.

"It is important for an exhibit designer to make an exhibit more accessible to the public, who can then begin to learn what ideas the curators are attempting to communicate. I have observed that an exhibit designer needs a graphic artist to make decisions about type treatment, type placement, logo development, and graphics.

"One of my goals this summer was to arrange portfolio reviews in the Washington, D.C., area and meet professional designers. Hank looked at my design portfolio and immediately recommended I speak with a colleague. This interview taught me a lot! I also had the opportunity to meet with the former director of design at the museum.

"I am scheduling an appointment with the assistant of exhibition design at the National Gallery. I have recorded suggestions from these reviews that will enable me to improve my portfolio and decide on a direction for my senior project. It has been valuable also in developing interviewing skills. I feel more confident about my work and have a clearer idea of what aspect of design I will follow as a career as a result of this internship."

Kendra graduated from Auburn University, then went to work at the Birmingham Museum of Art as a publications designer, designing all the printed promotional pieces that the museum used, such as invitations, newsletters, posters, and T-shirts. Kendra's next goal was to attend a master of fine arts program in design history.

A Small Museum

Nauvoo, Illinois, is a historic city on the banks of the Mississippi River, near the point where Iowa, Missouri, and Illinois meet. Fairly isolated, Nauvoo is 260 miles south of Chicago and about 170 miles north of St. Louis. Originally it had been a Sac and Fox Indian village, named Quashquema, for their chief. When Mormon founder Joseph Smith arrived in 1839, he called the site Nauvoo, from the old Hebrew word meaning "beautiful place."

The town is laid out like a mini-Williamsburg, with beautiful gardens and more than two dozen restored homes and shops open to the public. Early crafts have been given a second life, and skilled artisans give daily demonstrations. Many of the staff, including the director, guides, and caretakers, live on-site. The year-round population of Nauvoo numbers only about eleven hundred, and most of these residents work for one of the two main Mormon churches that share ownership of the town.

The Church of Jesus Christ of Latter-day Saints, with headquarters is in Salt Lake City, Utah, owns and operates the Visitors Center on the north side of town, as well as many other neighboring properties.

The Joseph Smith Historic Center on the south side of town is operated by the Reorganized Church of Latter-day Saints, whose headquarters is in Independence, Missouri. The Joseph Smith Historic Center has a Visitors Center that houses a greeting gallery, two theaters, and a small museum room displaying artifacts of the Smith family. There is also a library containing rare books of the period, along with reference books on the restoration and reconstruction of historic buildings and artifacts.

Visitors to the Joseph Smith Historic Center also tour the Joseph Smith Homestead, whose log cabin portion was built around 1803; the 1842 Mansion House; the Smith family cemetery; and the Joseph Smith Red Brick Store, which was reconstructed in 1979.

What It's Like to Be a Director at the Joseph Smith Historic Center

Don Albro was director of historic sites at the Joseph Smith Historic Center until his retirement in 2000. He feels he was chosen for this position because of his long relationship with the church (he has been an ordained minister since 1955), his interest and studies in history, and his management skills gained while in charge of an extensive sales force in private industry.

As director, Don was responsible for a full-time secretary, two maintenance workers, eight student interns, and ten senior guides who worked on a volunteer basis. He coordinated the student intern program and volunteer guide staff and their training, as well as overseeing the historic properties and their upkeep, maintenance, and reconstruction. As director of a small museum, Don performed functions that would not normally fall under the director's realm in a larger organization. A typical day might also include the following tasks, which he said were his favorites:

- Conducting tours
- Assisting with cooking demonstrations at the site's Summer Kitchen
- Working in the gift shop or the Red Brick Store
- Repairing buildings
- Trimming trees, planting flowers, weeding, and cutting thirty-four acres of grass

Finding That Job

The *Official Museum Directory*, put out by the American Association of Museums, is a valuable resource found in the reference section of most libraries. In addition to its pages and pages of history museums and historic houses, buildings, and sites, it lists scores of historical and preservation societies, boards, agencies, councils, commissions, foundations, and research industries.

The American Association of Museums puts out a monthly newsletter, which lists employment opportunities and internships. Here are a few examples of the types of jobs advertised:

- **Historian II.** The state historical society of a northwest state is seeking a historian to manage the society's scholarly history magazine. Responsibilities include editing agency newsletters, developing materials for state historic sites, and providing assistance with planning the society's public programs. Minimum qualifications: M.A. in history, English, or journalism, plus proven experience in editing, design, and layout.
- **Museum Archivist.** A public museum in the Midwest is seeking a half-time archivist to manage its collection of materials related to local history. Minimum requirement: bachelor's degree in archives administration, U.S. history, or library science, and three years professional experience.
- **Director.** Seeking creative, energetic individual to oversee exciting historic house museum and garden. Responsibilities include collections management and exhibit and educational program development. Background in decorative arts and ability to work with board and volunteers important.
- **Site Director.** Famous American author's home needs site director to oversee all facets of historic site management, including staffing, interpretation, and event planning. Museum management degree or equivalent required, plus proven experience.
- **Intern.** A museum of archaeology and anthropology at an eastern university anticipates funding for a nine-month collections management internship. Interns participate in a comprehensive training program and supervise volunteers

in storage renovations and computer inventory of a
designated collection. Candidate should be interested in a
museum career and have a background in
archaeology/anthropology or museum studies.

For More Information

Listed below are three useful reports published by the American
Association of Museums, whose address and website can be found
in Appendix A.

Careers in Museums: A Variety of Vocations. Gives a broad
overview of professional career opportunities in museums,
suggests educational qualifications and experience for specific
positions, and provides information on how to obtain
internships. It also lists job placement resources.

Museum Studies Programs: Guide to Evaluation. Answers
questions about the curricula and quality of museum studies
programs.

*Graduate Training in Museum Studies: What Students Need to
Know.* Helps future professionals assess training options in
museum studies, including certification, advanced degrees,
and internships.

CHAPTER FIVE

Jobs for Structure Lovers

Preserving the Past

ove of historic buildings and architecture is shared by all architectural historians, architectural conservators, curators of structures, restoration architects, and other preservationists. Some may specialize in a particular period or style, fascinated particularly by Victorian houses, Manhattan brownstones, federalist mansions, or frontier frame farmhouses and barns. Most, however, are generalists, possessing knowledge and appreciation that spans continents and centuries.

These professionals are good researchers, architects, and artists who have a breadth of highly developed skills and share a dedication to the environment as well as to the preservation of history.

The activity of preservation can be broken down into several different categories:

- **Adaptive Reuse**—providing a new function for older structures that would otherwise be demolished. For example, a defunct mill is converted into an office building or a college.
- **Architectural Conservation**—using special techniques to halt further deterioration of building materials.
- **Restoration** (often prefaced with *Historical* or *Architectural*)—involving the meticulous return of a

building to its former appearance at a particular period in
history.
- **Rehabilitation or Renovation**—altering or upgrading
existing buildings and structures.

Architectural Conservators

Architectural conservators are not necessarily registered architects. They may have started out in the construction and contracting field, gaining specialized technical experience in problems that
occur with historic buildings. Some of these problems involve the
historic building fabric, such as cracks in foundations and walls,
water seepage, and cleaning and repair of the building.

Architectural conservators understand how buildings were constructed during earlier periods and know what kinds of complica-
tions result from the natural course of time and different climatic
and environmental conditions. They are familiar with building
materials, roofs, windows, exterior cladding, and various reconstruction types, such as wood-frame or masonry-clad structures.

Architectural conservators are also sometimes known as curators of structures.

What It's Like to Be a Structures Curator

Curators of structures work for art and history museums, living
history museums, and historical societies and associations. A
curator, in the general sense of the word, is a caregiver—someone
who takes care of, for example, art collections, research documents, textiles, or historic buildings.

Mark Fortenberry was the curator of structures with the Nantucket Historical Association from 1987 to 1994. He was responsible for the maintenance of the twelve different historic sites owned
and operated by the association, and he was specifically concerned
with architectural accuracy in terms of period. He also supervised
contractors and technicians hired to perform restorations and

construct reproductions. Some of the sites included the Oldest House, the Hadwen House, the Thomas Macy Warehouse, and the Old Mill. Mark talked about his former duties:

"When I first came to the association, I was involved heavily with fieldwork—replication and carpentry. As curator of structures, I worked more on an administrative level; I coordinated the restoration and repair work that goes on in the buildings. This involved meetings with architects, long-range planning, scheduling, and budgets. We continually upgraded each building as the budget permitted; we not only did routine maintenance, but we handled more serious work in terms of maintaining the historical integrity of the building and its presentation to the public. We were also concerned with safety to the public, security systems, providing handicap access, and environmental upgrading such as cooling and heating systems.

"I also worked closely with the different offices within the association. For example, we refurbished the interior of one of the house museums, so I coordinated with the curator of collections on that.

"My job was multifaceted. Because we were a relatively small organization—sixteen or so full-time professionals—I had to be prepared to take on a wide range of tasks. Normally, a better-funded organization would have an architect on staff, would have someone else in charge of security, but those duties all fell under my umbrella."

Background. Mark grew up in Nantucket, a town where every building is on the National Register of Historic Places. It's easy to see how his interest in history developed, under those conditions. Before joining the Nantucket Historical Association as a full-time employee, Mark was self-employed as a restoration carpenter for more than twenty years. He also worked with the Massachusetts Historical Commission and did volunteer work for the Nantucket Historical Commission, designing exhibits and constructing showcases, among other things. He has always enjoyed working on older buildings.

On the island, there is a strong sensitivity toward maintaining the feeling that Nantucket is from another time. With Mark's experience and love of Nantucket, he was a natural to work with the Nantucket Historical Association as a full-time curator.

Restoration Architect

A restoration architect or an architect specializing in historic preservation has much of a general architect's experience. He or she understands how to plan spaces, how to organize construction materials, and how to put together construction documents.

The difference between a general architect and a restoration architect is that the latter's work experience has primarily been focused on historic buildings. In addition, the restoration architect has a specialized knowledge and understanding of federal, state, and local regulations with regard to historic preservation and is also aware of the standards set by the particular style of architecture.

What It's Like to Be a Restoration Architect

Peter Benton earned a bachelor's degree in architecture in 1972 from the University of Virginia in Charlottesville. He worked for several years for various firms in Philadelphia and Washington, D.C., then went on to complete his master's degree in architecture from the University of Pennsylvania in 1979.

Peter became a senior associate with John Milner Associates, Inc., a midsize architectural firm in West Chester, Pennsylvania, that specialized in historic preservation. He joined the staff in 1984 and worked on a variety of projects over the next two decades. Peter talked about his profession:

"Initially, I had relatively little training in preservation, but I was exposed to the idea of ecological planning at the University of

Pennsylvania. I saw the philosophical connection between an ecological approach to the landscape and to the buildings, and that
led me to historic preservation. I went to work for four or five
years for an ecological planning firm, and it was there my interest
developed further.

"I've been responsible for all sorts of properties—anything
from small, privately owned residential-scale houses from the
eighteenth century to high-style nineteenth-century mansions. In
addition, I've worked with historic commercial and industrial
buildings from the nineteenth century, restoring them or practicing what we call adaptive reuse. For example, we recently converted an old mill into an office building and a farmhouse into a
meeting facility. Another category I've worked with includes mon-
umental buildings, such as a city hall or large federal buildings."

The Nine Steps in a Restoration Project. Restoration projects can be major undertakings, and it is important for everyone
involved to understand and to share the same goals.

1. The restoration architect first meets with the client and
   determines what his or her goals are for the property.
2. The restoration architect does an "existing conditions
   analysis" of the site, looks at the historical development of
   the building over time, and takes photographs, field
   measurements, and written notes.
3. Next, the restoration architect creates a schematic plan,
   making preliminary drawings and sketches, and presents a
   design to the client for the client's approval. This stage may
   take several weeks or more, depending on the complexity of
   the project. Conversation, adjustments, and more
   conversation may also take place, until the design meets all
   requirements.
4. Once the client has approved the design for the project,
   the restoration architect produces an outline of the scope

of the work and calculates and presents an order-of-magnitude cost estimate.

5. After that stage is approved, the next phase is to work on design development documents. This involves the use of more detailed drawings and can take from six to eight weeks or more.

6. During the next several weeks, construction documents, including drawings and specifications, are produced.

7. A bidding phase is begun, and, following its completion, the contractor will have been selected from those who bid.

8. Construction plans are carefully reviewed before any construction is actually begun.

9. The restoration architect makes frequent visits to the site while the project is in progress. Construction time varies but can take months or a year or more, depending upon the scope of the project.

Salaries. Someone fresh from graduate school can expect to earn from $30,000 to $40,000 per year, depending upon the size of the firm, the importance of the project, and the region of the country. According to the 2008–2009 edition of the U.S. Department of Labor's *Occupational Outlook Handbook*: "Median annual earnings of wage-and-salary architects were $64,150 in May 2006. The middle 50 percent earned between $49,780 and $83,450. The lowest 10 percent earned less than $39,420, and the highest 10 percent earned more than $104,970. Those just starting their internships can expect to earn considerably less."

Advancement depends upon ability and accomplishments. An experienced architect with five years or more at the project manager level could expect to earn about $65,000 a year in a midsize firm. Those with specializations in demand can earn more. Most firms offer paid internships for graduate students.

Salaries in Canadian firms are usually slightly higher, but the cost of living in urban areas of the country is higher also.

Architectural Historian

Most architectural historians are primarily historians who have a specific interest in architecture. They are generally not registered architects. They often work with restoration architects, however, conducting specialized investigations and performing all the research necessary to get a restoration project under way. They dig up a building's history—when it was constructed, what its original purpose was, how long it was vacant, whether any changes had been made. They then put together a historic structures report for the architect who wants to make his or her restoration work as accurate as possible. Architectural historians can work in academic settings, for private architectural firms, and for government agencies concerned with historic preservation. The minimum requirement for an architectural historian is an undergraduate degree in history or architectural history, although most positions require a graduate degree.

Historical Interiors Designer

To achieve complete authenticity, the interior of a historic building must be given as much attention as the exterior, especially if the building will be used as a museum open to the public. Historic interiors designers can be architects or specially trained professionals. They must be experienced in the investigation, documentation, research, and analysis of the lighting, furnishings, finishes, and decorative arts of building interiors. Historic interiors specialists generally work as part of a team with the restoration architect and conservator.

Close-Up: The National Trust for Historic Preservation

The National Trust for Historic Preservation is a nonprofit organization with more than 270,000 members. Most of the National Trust's funding comes from membership dues, corporation and foundation grants, endowment income, and merchandise sales. Federal funding was discontinued in 1998, but the trust has continued and grown under private funding.

The National Trust's mission is, in part, to preserve and revitalize the livability of U.S. communities by leading the nation in saving America's historic environments. It provides technical advice and financial assistance to nonprofit organizations and public agencies engaged in preservation, as well as to the general public. The National Trust also acts as an advocate for protection of the country's heritage in the courts and with legislative and regulatory agencies.

The National Trust believes that the employment outlook in the historic preservation field has grown dramatically since the early 1980s. Its concerns have enlarged from a relatively small number of historic sites, museums, and buildings to historic neighborhoods, commercial districts, and rural landscapes.

The growing sophistication of the field is reflected in the greater diversity of professionals who contribute to preservation work. Historians, curators, and other museum professionals are now joined by architects, lawyers, designers, realtors, planners, developers, mortgage lenders, and others. Once found working only in museums, libraries, and historical societies, preservationists now are also employed in real estate firms that specialize in historical properties and in financial institutions that invest in older neighborhoods.

The National Trust employs many specialists in its national office in Washington, D.C., and in its seven regional offices. In addition, the National Trust owns and operates eighteen historic house museums. It also publishes *Preservation* magazine, which is distributed to members. To join, contact:

National Trust for Historic Preservation
1785 Massachusetts Avenue NW
Washington, DC 20036
www.preservationnation.org

For More Information

You may wish to review the *Guide to Graduate Degree Programs in Architectural History*, compiled by Richard Betts, available online at the website of the Society of Architectural Historians. For more information, contact:

Society of Architectural Historians
1365 North Astor Street
Chicago, IL 60610
www.sah.org

CHAPTER SIX

Jobs in Historical Societies

Explaining the Past

Preservation boards and historical societies are dedicated to the mission of preserving, protecting, defending, and promoting the cultural, social, economic, environmental, and architectural integrity of their particular districts or historic sites. These boards and societies offer full-time employment or volunteer opportunities for most of the career categories discussed in this book. Architectural historians, archivists, restoration architects, researchers, design experts, curators, information officers, and administrators work as a team to achieve their goals.

Working for Historical Societies

Salaried jobs with preservation boards and historical societies are fairly limited. Many boards and societies are membership funded; others may receive government or private grants to carry on their work. The better-funded operations are able to hire specialists to work in their particular fields. Boards and societies with limited funds rely heavily on professionals willing to volunteer their time. The few paid employees take on a variety of tasks that span various career categories.

What It's Like to Be an Information Officer with the Miami Design Preservation League

Although George Neary's official title was administrative director of the Miami Design Preservation League, he also functioned as the sole full-time information officer for the league's Art Deco District. He earned his bachelor's degree in history at St. Anselm College in Manchester, New Hampshire, in 1970.

After teaching for many years, he moved to Miami and started with the Miami Design Preservation League as a volunteer in September 1991. In March 1992, he was hired as a full-time employee. In 1999, George went on to become the director of cultural tourism with the Greater Miami Convention and Visitors Bureau. George talked about his former job:

"It's a membership-funded organization, operating solely on membership dues, conducting tours, and putting on special events throughout the year. My assistant and I were the league's only paid employees. Everyone else was a volunteer. We had more than forty volunteers, which included a cadre of dedicated tour guides and office helpers. We also had the chairperson and the board members and various committee heads and members—all volunteer professionals.

"The most important task we focused on was the preservation of the Art Deco District. Our governmental affairs committee worked with the city on zoning and other issues to protect the district from demolition or misuse. We also had an executive committee, an architectural task force, an archivist, educational committees, tour committees, special events committees, historians, and writers.

"Most of my time was spent in the role of information officer, working with the public. I made sure all members were kept informed of what was going on in the district. I handled huge mailings and sent out press releases or called the radio stations when special shows were scheduled. When we were putting on a major event, such as the Art Deco Weekend, I had to make sure that everything ran smoothly. I was also involved with budgeting, assigning tasks to staff members, and supervising tour guides. Occasionally I gave tours myself to special-interest groups from out of town.

"I also worked as a liaison with the city, state, and federal governments. We rallied the troops, lobbying to halt demolition permits and getting laws passed to protect the district.

"I arranged for monthly speakers and encouraged our members to attend. The members were very important to the whole operation. When they joined the league, their dues supported our activities. Members were entitled to certain privileges, such as receiving the newsletter we published, invitations to monthly gatherings and lectures, and our annual meeting, which was also open to the public."

Tour Guides and Docents

Although the titles vary in different establishments, there is little if any difference between the role of a tour guide and that of a docent. Depending on the place of employment, tour guides may or may not be in costume. They are not primarily responsible for conducting their own research and do not usually portray one particular character, although they may be expected to carry out these roles in some institutions. Tour guides don't usually speak from a prepared script, and they must have broad, general knowledge of the historical area and period being emphasized.

Tour guides may be employed by the federal or a state government, by historical societies, by museums, or by a private enterprise. Some are self-employed.

Tour guides may ride in the front of a bus or boat, microphone in hand; be stationed in a particular building or site, such as a church, museum, or fort; may share space with visitors in a horse-drawn carriage or buggy; or may lead visitors around on historical walking tours.

What It's Like to Be a Tour Guide in Miami Beach's Art Deco District

Many people used to think of Miami Beach as a place populated solely by retired folks. For a long time, Collins Avenue and Ocean Drive, packed with residential hotels and condominiums, did cater to the over-sixty set. But in recent years, the demographics, as well as the topography, have been changing.

Jeff Donnelly became a volunteer tour guide for the Miami Design Preservation League. He knew the area as well as anyone. Monday through Friday he taught history and political science at a local day school in Dade County. But on Saturday mornings, he donned his Panama hat and walking shoes and took groups on ninety-minute strolling tours through Miami Beach's restored Art Deco District.

"Miami Beach is an exciting place to live these days," Jeff explained. "Young professionals, artists, models, movie production people—they're all flocking here now. We've become very chic."

After cautioning the twenty or so people in his group—from New York, Texas, Colorado, and nearby Fort Lauderdale—about the strong Florida sun ("If anyone feels dehydrated, please raise your hand before you pass out"), he provided them with more than just a passing glimpse into Miami's colorful mystique.

"As elderly residents moved into nursing homes or passed away, investors and developers began buying up and renovating the run-down buildings," he said. "In the process, they uncovered the fantasy seaside resort that had first inspired the original boom back in the 1920s and 1930s.

"There were five major architects responsible for the district. Although they were commercial competitors, they were also coffee-klatch friends. If someone's building supplies hadn't arrived on time or if someone ran short, they lent materials back and forth. This, of course, explains the high level of style consistency throughout the district."

The old establishments, once painted white and only trimmed with powder blue, aquamarine, or the peaches and pinks of the local flamingos, now have received fresh face-lifts and glow with a brighter and more contemporary palette. Bands of lavender, blue, yellow, aqua, and a whole spectrum of pinks whimsically decorate oceanfront hotels, sidewalk cafés, model agencies, and apartment buildings.

Miami Beach can boast one of the largest concentrations of art deco buildings in the country: more than eight hundred structures contribute to the historic architectural nature of the city's Art Deco District. The result is an effervescent urban streetscape, with the promise of campy humor and fun.

"You'd almost expect to see flappers strolling arm in arm or Al Capone roaring up in his jalopy," observed one member of the tour group. Indeed, it's rumored that Al Capone often ate at the Park Central Hotel on Ocean Drive, with his bodyguards perched on the overhead balcony for protection. Whether that story is true or not, the gangster movie *Scarface* was filmed there.

Art deco combines elements of art moderne, cubism, futurism, and expressionism, in a bold and linear style that originated in Paris and became popular in the 1920s and 1930s. When it was built, Miami Beach's architecture was considered ultramodern; the goal was to be futuristic, to look ahead. After the shock and horror of World War I, which had destroyed much of Europe and affected civilization all over the world, and, later, the sudden downturn of the stock market crash, the architects and designers wanted to convey the message that happy days were coming.

Today, however, the art deco area is not a historic district that preservationists seek to preserve exactly as it was in the twenties and thirties. "We're not a Williamsburg," Jeff explained. "Our philosophy is what we call 'adaptive reuse'—[the] restoration projects focus on designs with contemporary uses. It allows for a larger variety of colors and for more of the surface areas to be given over to color."

Anyone who wants to renovate must bring their plans to the Miami Design Preservation League Review Board for approval. "The meetings are a great source of local entertainment," said Jeff. "The arguments over color choices are fascinating."

The Miami Design Preservation League was established in 1976 and is the oldest art deco organization in the world. For three years, the league cataloged the art deco– and Mediterranean revival–style buildings, earning a listing in the National Register of Historic Places. The league's main function after that was to guard against demolitions, incompatible construction, and false restorations.

"We don't want new construction to completely imitate the old style," Jeff said. "There's a Kentucky Fried Chicken that slipped by before the Review Board was established. It looks so much like a building from the twenties—it confuses people."

The hotels that line Ocean Drive are the real thing, however. Many were named after posh New York establishments to convey a sense of luxury—like The Ritz and Waldorf Towers. Some are named after the designers' family members, like the Victor and the Adrian.

It's not only the bright colors that attract the eye. Special attention to form, detail, and vertical and horizontal lines make up the art deco style. Buildings have varying themes: streamlined, rounded corners accented with "eyebrows," and needlelike finials pointing skyward. The Breakwater Hotel's stylish lines were used in an early Buck Rogers film. Rare, etched-glass windows, fluted cornices, stepped rooflines, horizontal racing stripes, and nautical, art moderne porthole windows are like jewelry on the bodies of the buildings.

The Avalon Hotel added a special touch to complete its own pretty picture—a 1950 yellow-and-white Oldsmobile, rimmed with shiny chrome, is regularly parked in front of the yellow building.

A number of advertising and modeling agencies often used the hotel as a backdrop for photographic shoots. Any morning of the week, when the early eastern light splashes across the soft colors, five or six different photo shoots can be seen already in progress. Scenes from the TV show "Miami Vice" were frequently shot along Ocean Drive, where many celebrities visit.

Special events regularly add even more life to this spirited district. One of those events is the Art Deco Weekend, held annually on the second weekend of January. It relives the days of the big bands, speakeasies, and street theater against Miami Beach's classic art deco backdrop. Antique cars, period artwork, collectibles, and memorabilia carry visitors back in time to the Roaring Twenties.

Nighttime brings a new dimension to the Art Deco District. Neon tube lighting was first invented in the late 1930s, and Ocean Drive was a showcase for this exciting new discovery.

"It must have been a magical experience for those seeing the glowing, colorful lights against the glass block for the first time," said Jeff.

Many of the lobbies inside the hotels are equally magical. Original murals and paintings of the era adorn the walls, and colorful inlaid terrazzo stone chips decorate the floors in geometric patterns.

Jeff pointed out the last stop, the Blackstone Hotel, where George Gershwin reputedly wrote *Porgy and Bess*, and then he steered his group back to the Art Deco Welcome Center.

"It's ironic, really," Jeff concluded. "We've put a lot of effort into preserving an era that actually stood for forward movement, growth, and development. But the architects of the time hit on just the right note for Miami Beach. What was beautiful then is even more beautiful now. It's certainly worth preserving."

For more information on the Art Deco District, contact:

Miami Design Preservation League
PO Box 190180
Miami Beach, FL 33119
www.mdpl.org

What It's Like to Be a Docent for the Nantucket Historical Association

Jeremy Slavitz was a paid docent for the Nantucket Historical Association. Although he grew up in a location noted for its historical significance, it wasn't until he attended college that his interest in history developed. He wasn't sure what he wanted to do, so he enrolled in a variety of classes. The history courses interested him the most, and he discovered it was important to work in a discipline he enjoyed. He graduated from the University of Massachusetts, Amherst, in 1992 with a bachelor's degree in history, specializing in naval history. The summer of 1992 was his first season as a docent. He later picked up additional responsibilities over the years. He became docent trainer, worked with the educational programs for children, and is now coordinator of public programs. Jeremy talked about his former job:

"What I liked most about working as a docent for the historical association was that it gave me a chance to work in history, but I wasn't stuck in a closet doing research. I could get out and talk to people. I gave information every day, struggling to make it interesting for people. I enjoyed the challenge.

"The docents always work in pairs, and that's one of the other aspects that helped to make the job fun. There were several other college students employed as well as the older residents. We alternated taking guests through. On a rainy day, we were very busy, with not much time to rest. When the sun was out, most visitors to Nantucket headed for the beach. Then the day at the association went a bit slower.

"The docents with the historical association try to portray our museums throughout their history. Rather than just identifying a certain object, a chair or a table, we tried to give visitors a more three-dimensional picture of the people who were living there through various time periods, as well as the different ways the building was used.

"For example, one of the properties I worked in is Nantucket's Oldest House. It was built in 1686 by Jethro Coffin. He was a wealthy businessman, and at that time his house was one of the largest on the island and was considered the most prestigious. We showed the house as it was then, and we showed it as it was during the eighteenth century after another owner, Nathaniel Paddack, bought it. He was a weaver, and he worked on his loom in the home. During his time, as the island population grew, the house was considered to be of modest proportions and no longer held the same prestige. We also showed the house as it is now, a small structure with three rooms on the ground floor and two rooms upstairs.

"I didn't work from a prepared script. There is a general guideline to follow, but I had the freedom to tailor my presentation based on who was visiting. One summer, there was a local boy whose parents were members of the historical association. They gave him their pass, which allows admission to about twelve different properties, put him on his bicycle, and sent him on his way. He would bring his friends, and over the course of the summer, they followed me around to the different sites where I worked. They'd wait until most of the other visitors had left, so I could show them parts of the buildings they would find the most interesting. They peered up chimneys and climbed through root cellars and figured out how the loom worked. They had a great time. Someone else would have an entirely different interest, so I would focus on another aspect for them."

Hours and Salary. Jeremy put in as many hours as possible as a docent and usually worked a forty-hour week spread over six days. Because one of the museums is open at night, he was also on duty for some evening hours.

He was paid $6 an hour when he worked as a docent, but later docents were paid $11 per hour.

Training. "The training process was very enjoyable. In each museum there is a book that has been put together that includes all the known information about the house or building. On top of that, there are people here who have done this for years, so a lot of the training has to do with oral history. New docents are learning from people who have learned from people before them. Some of the older docents have lived on the island all of their lives, and they can pass down the history, as well as their own experiences with the property."

For more information on Nantucket history, contact:

Nantucket Historical Association
PO Box 1016
Nantucket, MA 02554
www.nha.org

CHAPTER SEVEN

Jobs for Diggers

Uncovering the Past

Treasure is the goal, and digging is the means to arrive there. Most history professionals are diggers—both literally and figuratively: they dig up information from the past. Some dig through mounds of dirt for baubles and bones and priceless evidence of past civilizations; others dig through dusty archives in softly lit old courthouses and peer into microfiche readers at infinite numbers of worn file cards and copies of ships' logs.

Many professions are involved in this kind of historical work, including archaeologists, archivists, genealogists, and historical anthropologists, among others.

Archaeologist

Archaeology is one subdivision of the field of anthropology. Archaeologists study the artifacts of past cultures to learn about their histories, customs, and living habits. They survey and excavate archaeological sites, recording and cataloging their finds. By careful analysis, archaeologists reconstruct earlier cultures and determine their influences on the present.

Archaeological sites are the physical remains of past civilizations. They can include building debris and the items found inside, in addition to trash and garbage. Usually these sites have been buried by other, later human activity or by various natural processes.

Excavation of these sites is a painstaking process conducted by professionals using modern techniques. Because these sites are so fragile, the very nature of excavating destroys some information. With this in mind, archaeologists are careful to dig only as much as is needed to answer important questions. Frequently, archaeologists concentrate their work on sites slated for destruction to make room for new highway or building construction.

Archaeologists work in a variety of settings: universities and colleges, private schools, and museums; for various government agencies; and for construction companies and architectural firms. In these settings, they do a broad variety of work, including teaching, fieldwork, research, directing student work, developing displays and presentations, as well as excavating, surveying, classifying, analyzing, preserving, and storing artifacts and remains.

Working conditions for archaeologists vary considerably. At times they work under harsh conditions in the field, then have complete comfort indoors in offices and classrooms and labs when not in the field.

Archaeologists conducting fieldwork often work with several other professionals in a team effort. They are assisted by geologists, ethnologists, educators, anthropologists, ecologists, and aerial photographers.

In the field, archaeologists use a variety of tools on-site at a dig. These include measuring and mapping equipment, picks, shovels, trowels, wheelbarrows, sifting boxes, pressure sprayers, brushes, cameras, laptop computers, recorders, and labeling and storage supplies. Archaeologists also make drawings and sketches on-site and take detailed notes.

What It Takes to Become an Archaeologist

Do you have what it takes to become an archaeologist? Take this self-evaluation quiz and get some clues. For each of the following statements, ask yourself if it describes you:

1. I have above-average academic ability.
2. I have an avid interest in science and history.
3. Hours of strenuous activity (lifting, carrying, shoveling) do not pose a problem for me.
4. I have been told I have leadership qualities.
5. The idea of continuing study throughout my career appeals to me.
6. I am a logical and analytical thinker.
7. I enjoy working independently.
8. I function well as part of a team.
9. I believe professional ethics should be strictly adhered to.
10. I can live under primitive conditions in remote areas.

To consider yourself a potential archaeologist, you must have answered yes for every statement. Even with just one negative answer, you might want to reconsider your choice of field. Archaeology is an extremely rigorous and competitive profession.

Education

To qualify as a professional archaeologist, graduate study leading to a master's degree is necessary. A doctoral degree is often preferable. Most graduate programs in archaeology are found in anthropology departments. There are about fifty universities with advanced archaeology degree programs. Find them online at Peterson's Graduate Planner, www.petersons.com.

To gain the necessary background at the undergraduate level, students need to pursue a study of anthropology, history, art, geology, or a related field. At the graduate level, students following a course in archaeology would also include cultural and physical anthropology and linguistics in their curriculum.

Job Opportunities

Relatively few openings exist in the field of teaching archaeology. Recently, however, more federal grants and contracts have been made available for archaeological fieldwork and research. A lot of this work is being conducted in the western and southwestern states, such as Colorado, Arizona, and New Mexico. Particularly in northwestern New Mexico, there is a strong industry developing resources such as gas and oil. Under the jurisdiction of the federal Bureau of Land Management, professional archaeologists must be hired to clear the site before gas lines or wells can be put in.

In Colorado, the building of a reservoir on the Dolores River uncovered hundreds of archaeological sites, necessitating a great deal of archaeological work. The project, as the largest on the continent, brought many archaeologists to that area.

Interested history buffs who don't desire full-time professional careers as archaeologists but would like to experience archaeological work can find many opportunities to try their hands at a dig. If you are willing to invest your time—and in some cases, your money—you can easily find professionally supervised archaeological investigations taking on volunteers. These are regularly listed in *Archaeology* magazine. A few other places to contact are provided below:

Crow Canyon Archaeological Center
23390 Road K
Cortez, CO 81321
www.crowcanyon.org

> *Crow Canyon provides high-quality instruction and hosts important guest lecturers, such as Dr. Donny George Youkhanna, former director of National Museum of Iraq in Baghdad, who described the looting of more than two thirds of the antiquities and the destruction of the museum during the Iraq War and warned everyone that collections must be protected, worldwide, against natural disasters and unexpected social chaos.*

Earthwatch Institute
3 Clock Tower Place, Suite 100
Box 75
Maynard, MA 01754
www.earthwatch.org

*This well-known center in Massachusetts has fostered global
awareness and international exchange.*

Center for American Archeology
PO Box 366
Kampsville, IL 62053
www.caa-archeology.org

*The center provides hands-on, on-site experience with expert
instruction for professional and avocational archaeologists and their
families. It's famous for its work at the Koster Site in Greene County,
Illinois, near the confluence of the Illinois and Mississippi rivers.*

Close-Up: Crow Canyon Archaeological Center

Crow Canyon is a nonprofit research and educational institution
funded by tuition fees, donations, and federal grants. It features an
eighty-acre campus in southwestern Colorado, near Mesa Verde
National Park, with a staff of about fifty archaeologists, educators,
and support personnel. In addition to its own research, the institution instructs participants, both adults and children, who want
to learn about archaeology. From junior-high age on, participants
are taken into the field and taught excavation, recording, and documentation techniques. They also work in the lab learning analysis techniques and methods for cleaning artifacts.

Children too young to work in the field can still participate in a simulated dig in a lab that Crow Canyon has set up for that purpose. There they can learn the same excavating techniques as they sift through large, shallow sandboxes where artifacts and walls and other features are buried, as they would be in the field.

Participants come from all over the United States on educational vacations and stay for three- to five-day programs. Crow Canyon also works with about a dozen graduate students of archaeology a year, providing rewarding internships.

During the summer months, participants sleep in cabins, tents, or hogans—circular Navajo-style structures.

In Montezuma County, where Crow Canyon is located, there are more than one hundred thousand archaeological sites. Crow Canyon professionals work at two different nearby sites—Sand Canyon Pueblo and Castle Rock Pueblo, both on Bureau of Land Management land. The sites were once Anasazi Indian villages. The Anasazi were the predecessors of present-day Pueblo Indians and lived in this area and throughout the Southwest from the sixth century until about the year 1300. The Crow Canyon researchers are focusing on exactly when the Anasazi left and why. They are also investigating the political and social systems of the Anasazi.

What It's Like to Be a Field Anthropologist at Crow Canyon

Kristin Kuckelman became a field anthropologist at Crow Canyon Archaeological Center, following an interest that began when she was a child. Kristin's father was in the U.S. Air Force, and she traveled with her parents around the world. They were interested in different cultures and in archaeology as well, and they passed those interests on to their daughter. When it came time to go to college, Kristin was naturally drawn to the anthropology program. Kristin talked about her job:

"I love the variety of it. I enjoy working outdoors; I enjoy writing. And with any kind of research, there's the excitement of discovery. You're trying to solve problems, you're trying to find things out, you're trying to learn something new. And, basically, every time you go in the field, you hope you're going to learn something about a culture that no one knew before. You don't know what that's going to be; you never really know how it's going to turn out or what you're going to find.

"The sites in this particular area are very easy to discern. They have many hundreds of masonry rooms with, even after centuries, telltale piles of rubble and thousands of artifacts scattered about the ground. Just from walking around the modern ground surface, you can see the tops of the walls and the depressions in the ground indicating the subterranean chambers.

"Sand Canyon covers about four acres. Castle Rock is smaller, close to three acres, and is situated around the base of a butte, a small flat-topped mountain.

"Because of the subterranean chambers, we sometimes have to dig down to two-and-a-half to three meters to find the actual floor of the structure. The surface rooms are shallower, but we can still have a meter, a meter-and-a-half filled in.

"We've found lithic artifacts, which are artifacts made out of stone, such as spear and arrow points, and sandstone tools for grinding grain. We've also found tens of thousands of pottery fragments—very rarely do we find a piece that is still intact. And very rarely do we engage in refitting, trying to piece the shards together. With so many pieces scattered over the ground, it would take many years, be very, very expensive, and would certainly drive someone crazy!

"Beginning with the first week in May, which is the start of our field season, my partner and I head out to the site, set up equipment, and make sure we have the areas we want excavated all laid out and prepared. We take care of all our paperwork and any mapping we have to do so we're ready for participants to begin digging.

"During the digging season, we take participants out two or three days a week, but the first full day is spent on campus. Our educators give them a full orientation about archaeology in general. Out in the field, we give them a site tour to give them a background on what it is we're going to be digging, why we're digging, what we're trying to learn. We then give them tools and individual instruction and place them, either individually or in pairs, at the particular places we want excavated.

"Basically, we move dirt and put it in a bucket and then take it to a screening station, which is a quarter-inch mesh screen. The dirt gets sifted through the screen to make sure we're not losing any artifacts. Everybody has a different bag to keep artifacts from each excavation area separate.

"Near the end of the season, we have quite a bit of documentation and mapping to do, and we wash and analyze the artifacts. When we're finished with them, most of the artifacts are put in storage, though a few are rotated as exhibits at the Anasazi Heritage Center, a federally run, curatorial facility.

"Then we have to fill the areas we've dug back in with all the screened dirt and rocks we originally dug out. The idea is if you were to walk across the site a year later, you'd never know there had been an excavation there. For safety reasons, we can't leave gaping holes in the land, and in terms of conservation, to leave a pit open to the elements would damage the site.

"Before we close it back up, we line the pit with landscaping fabric to protect it and to provide a clue in case future archaeologists are digging there but do not have access to our notes and maps. The lining would show them the site had already been excavated. There are so many sites, and to keep a site open and developed for public exhibit, as has been done at Mesa Verde, would be extremely expensive. It would also be very hard on the architecture itself. Constant maintenance would have to be performed or everything would eventually deteriorate.

"During the winter, we write up in report form everything we learned the previous summer. We also write articles for professional journals and present papers at archaeological conferences across the country."

Background. Kristin graduated in 1975 with a bachelor's degree in anthropology and psychology from Colorado Women's College (which has now merged with the University of Denver). She earned her master's degree in anthropology with a concentration in archaeology from the University of Texas at Austin in 1977.

Further Reading

The following publications, though not available in every local library, can be found in most university libraries or in large public libraries.

PROFESSIONAL JOURNALS AND PERIODICALS

American Antiquity (Society for American Archaeology)

Archaeological Fieldwork Opportunities Bulletin (Archaeological Institute of America). You can search the online version of the bulletin at www.archaeological.org. The bulletin is a comprehensive guide to excavations, field schools, and special programs throughout the world with openings for volunteers, students, staff, and technicians.

Archaeology (Archaeological Institute of America)

Historical Archaeology (Society for Historical Archaeology)

Journal of Anthropological Archaeology (Elsevier)

Journal of Field Archaeology (Boston University)

National Geographic (National Geographic Society)

North American Archaeologist (Baywood Publishing Company)

Scientific American

Smithsonian (Smithsonian Institution)

Summer Field School List (American Anthropological Association)

BOOKS

Archaeology: A Brief Introduction, 9th ed., by Brian M. Fagan (Englewood Cliffs, NJ: Prentice Hall, 2005).

Archaeology: Theories, Methods, and Practice, 5th ed., by Colin Renfrew and Paul Bahn (New York: Thames and Hudson, 2008).

. . . .

Archivist

It is estimated that there are close to five thousand major archives in the United States. Each of the fifty states maintains government archives, as do most city and county governments. In addition, archives can be found in universities, historical societies, museums, libraries, and private businesses.

On the national level, the National Archives in Washington, D.C., looks after the records of the federal government. The Library of Congress provides information services to the U.S. Congress and technical services to all the libraries across the country.

Although archives are similar to libraries, there are distinct differences between the two. Libraries typically house materials that are published and were created with the express purpose of broad dissemination. Archives typically hold materials that were created in the course of carrying out some sort of business or activity but were never intended originally for public dissemination.

For example, in an archive you might find letters from a Civil War soldier to his family. He wrote about his experiences and feelings and to let his loved ones know that he was still alive, surviving this or that battle. He never would have imagined that his correspondence would be saved for public viewing. This gives his letters credibility, or integrity as a historical source. In contrast, the newspaper reporter covering the same battles is writing with a specific point of view for widespread publication, ultimately with the intention of selling newspapers.

Archives handle collections that chart the course of daily life for individuals and businesses. Some archives specifically look after materials created by their own institutions. The Coca-Cola Company, for example, set up an archive years ago to preserve a history of what the company business was and how it prospered. New companies set up archives to keep documented records. Other institutions, such as universities or museums, create archives that relate to their special research interests.

The material found in archives can be letters, personal papers, organizational records, and other documents. Archives created within the past one hundred years or so could also contain visual records such as photographs and postcards, as well as prints, drawings, and sketches. Today, archives also collect tape recordings, phonograph records, movie films, videotapes, and computer-stored information.

Because archives hold firsthand information, they are valuable to anyone with an interest in the people, places, and events of the past. This group includes genealogists, museum researchers, scholars, students, writers, and historians.

As with libraries and archives, there are distinct differences between librarians and archivists in the way they operate and the methods and techniques they use to handle material. The biggest single difference is that librarians look at materials they get on an item-by-item basis. Each book is a distinct entity evaluated separately from the other books. In an archive, a single letter would usually be part of a larger collection of letters. Archivists are interested in these as a group because one letter would only be a fragment. To really understand something about the past, the information needs to be synthesized and put together to form a collection.

Archivists provide a service to society by identifying and preserving materials with lasting value for the future. When archivists talk about their work, they discuss certain basic functions that are common to all archives. The numbers in parentheses designate the percentage of time usually spent on each duty in each of five areas:

1. Identification and acquisition of materials (10 percent)
2. Arrangement and description of collections (60 percent)
3. Preservation of collections (10 percent)

4. Reference services (15 percent)
5. Community outreach and public affairs (5 percent)

What It's Like to Be the Chief Archivist at the Museum of American History

John Fleckner came to the Smithsonian in 1982 with more than a decade's experience working as an archivist for the Wisconsin Historical Society. He is a past president of the Society of American Archivists and has acted as a consultant on many important archives projects, including the United Negro College Fund, the Vietnam History and Archives Project, and the Native American Archives Project.

John did his undergraduate work at Colgate University in Hamilton, New York, graduating in 1963 with a bachelor's degree, with honors, in history. He earned his master's degree in American history at the University of Wisconsin in 1965. He also amassed significant work toward a doctorate.

John is responsible for archives that acquire collections from the outside. These collections cover a wide range of subjects and are particularly strong in the areas of American music, advertising, and the history of technology.

At the Smithsonian, John was overseeing a professional staff of twelve archivists, three student interns, and close to twenty volunteers. He divided his time as follows:

1. Identification and acquisition of materials (15 percent)
2. Supervision (50 percent)
3. Reference services (10 percent)
4. Administration, meetings, budget, personnel (15 percent)
5. Outreach and public affairs (10 percent)

John talked about how he became an archivist:

"After too many years of graduate school, pursuing a vague notion of teaching college-level history, I realized that I really didn't want to teach. I was so naive, it took a university career counselor to recognize that my history background might be any-thing other than an economic liability. Leaning back in her chair, she pointed out her office window to the Wisconsin Historical Society just across the street, and she directed me to a recently established graduate program in archives administration. The instructor would make no promises about the prospects for a job, but with a sly smile he offered that all his previous students were working. I didn't need a weatherman—as they said in those days, the early 1970s—to tell me which way the wind was blowing.

"So, it was an accident in good guidance that got me in the door. But it was the experience of doing archival work—begin-ning with the simplest class exercises and then a formal intern-ship—that sealed it for me. I loved the combination of handicraft and analytical work, and I loved the intense, intimate contact with the 'stuff' of history. Before I completed my internship, I knew I wanted to be an archivist.

"Previously, as a graduate student, of course I had done some research in archives—at the Library of Congress, the College of William and Mary, and especially the State Historical Society. But the archivists had taken all the fun out of it. The materials were antiseptically put in folders, boxed, and listed. Wheeled out on carts, they were like cadavers to be dissected by first-year medical students. On occasion I even donned white gloves. The docu-ments always seemed lifeless.

"Later, as a would-be archivist, they thrilled me. I was in charge; I would evaluate their significance, determine their order, describe their contents, and physically prepare them for their permanent resting places.

"Still, it was not so much this heady feeling of control that awed me but more the mystery, the possibilities of the records them-selves. My judgments would be critical to building paths to the records for generations of researchers, across the entire spectrum of topics, and into unknown future time.

"The archival enterprise held another attractive feature for me. For all the opportunity to reconstruct the past captured in these documents, and to imagine the future research they might support, I had a well-defined task to accomplish, a product to produce, techniques and methods for proceeding, and standards against which my work would be judged. There was rigor and discipline; this was real work. And, as good fortune would have it, I soon was getting paid to do it."

Education

People get into the archives profession in a variety of traditional and unusual ways. Often in a small town, an archive is a closet in the back room of a local historical society's office. Someone volunteers to put it all together, perhaps the oldest person in the community with a strong interest in the area's history.

The standard way to become an archivist is to have an undergraduate degree with a history background and a graduate degree at least at the master's level that would involve specific course work in archives. Thirty to fifty programs are offered, usually in graduate library schools. The Society of American Archivists publishes a directory of these educational programs. Many archivists have master of library science (M.L.S.) degrees with a concentration in archives, but sometimes archives courses are taught in history departments.

Earnings

In May 2006, according to the *Occupational Outlook Handbook*, archivists earned a median annual salary of $40,730, with the lowest 10 percent earning less than $23,890 and the highest 10 percent earning more than $73,060.

Genealogist

The study of genealogy, tracing family histories, has recently become one of the most popular hobbies in the United States. Many genealogy hobbyists take this interest a step beyond tracing their own family histories and become self-employed genealogists, helping others to dig up their family trees. Some genealogists find work teaching their skills to others in adult education classes, editing genealogy magazines, or writing books or newspaper genealogy columns. Genealogists also are employed in historical societies and libraries with special genealogy rooms.

The Church of Jesus Christ of Latter-day Saints in Salt Lake City, for example, has a huge repository of family information in a subterranean library. The church employs genealogists all over the world, including those who have been accredited through its own program, on a list of freelance researchers. For more information, contact:

Family History Library
35 North West Temple Street, Room 344
Salt Lake City, UT 84150
www.familysearch.org

Most genealogists are not formally trained, though specializing in genealogy is possible through some university history and library science programs. In addition, a genealogist can become board certified. For information on certification requirements and procedures, write to:

Board for Certification of Genealogists
PO Box 14291
Washington, DC 20044
www.bcgcertification.org

Earnings

Salaries vary depending upon the institution where a genealogist is employed and upon the level of expertise he or she has reached. They are similar to researchers' and archivists' salaries and range from a little more than $20,000 a year to more than $70,000, with beginners starting at the low end and those with most qualifications and long years of experience earning at the top. It must be remembered that in small or nonprofit organizations, salaries may stay low because the budget is small to begin with.

Well-established, self-employed genealogists generally charge from $35 to $50 an hour and sometimes more. They do not necessarily work steady forty-hour weeks, nor can they keep all that they earn. Expenses are those of any small business and include office space, utilities, supplies, Internet and phone, equipment, advertising, insurance, and possibly financial, legal, and accounting fees. Taxes and other government payments, such as Social Security, must also be paid, usually on a quarterly basis.

Using any good search engine, check the Internet for *genealogists*. Compare the websites of a good sampling of genealogy services for their qualifications and certifications. Most professional genealogists' websites also provide detailed descriptions of fees, services, and how much time is involved.

Getting Started

The National Genealogical Society makes the following suggestions for beginners:

- **Question older family members.** Encourage them to talk about their childhoods and their relatives and listen carefully for clues they might inadvertently drop. Learn good interviewing techniques so you ask questions that elicit the most productive answers. Use a tape recorder and try to verify each fact through a separate source.
- **Visit your local library.** Become familiar with historical and genealogical publications (a few sources are provided at the end of this chapter and in Appendix D) and contact local historical societies and the state library and archives in your

state capital. Seek out any specialty ethnic or religious libraries and visit cemeteries.

- **Visit county courthouses and city hall archives.** Cultivate friendships with archivists, clerks, and librarians. Ask to see source records such as wills, deeds, marriage books, and birth and death certificates.

- **Correspond with others.** Write to other individuals or societies involved with the same families or regions. Contact embassies of other countries located in Washington, D.C. Restrict yourself to asking only one question in each letter you send. Include the information you have already uncovered and include a self-addressed, stamped envelope to encourage replies.

- **Become computer literate.** Members of the National Genealogical Society can participate in a special computer interest section. It encourages the use of computers in research, record management, and data sharing.

- **Keep painstaking records.** Use printed family group sheets or pedigree charts. Develop a well-organized filing system so you'll be able to easily find your information. Keep separate records for each family you research.

- **Write to the National Genealogical Society.** Take advantage of its forty-six-page book—*Beginners in Genealogy.* You can also enroll in a home-study course called American Genealogy: A Basic Course.

For more information, you can write to:

National Genealogical Society
3108 Columbia Pike, Suite 300
Arlington, VA 22204
www.ngsgenealogy.org

Additional information can be obtained from:

National Institute on Genealogical Research
PO Box 118
Greenbelt, MD 20768
www.rootsweb.ancestry.com/~natgenin

American Society of Genealogists
PO Box 519
Williamstown, MA 01267
www.fasg.org

For genealogical information in the United Kingdom, write to:

The National Archives – Kew
Richmond, Surrey TW9 4DU
England
www.nationalarchives.gov.uk

CHAPTER EIGHT

Writing and Photography

Documenting the Past

A s historians, our constant and compelling desire is to discover the truth and to tell the story. And where would that story be, after all, without the words and the pictures? We need to record it. Either we, ourselves, or other members on the team must be writers, artists, and photographers to record research findings and write reports, presentations, white papers, journal articles, books, and—sometimes, of course—grant proposals.

In addition, many innovative people have combined a love of history with talents or skills in other areas, such as fiction and nonfiction writing, advertising, public relations, marketing, and filmmaking. With a good imagination and a lot of drive and persistence, a dedicated history buff with writing or artistic skills can create a related career.

Writing

Here are a few successful ventures that might spark some ideas of your own.

What It's Like to Be a Desktop Publisher

Prudy Taylor Board, a published author, creative writing instructor, and staff writer for her local newspaper, established a sideline called Prudy's Press. She researched and self-published pamphlets covering the historic sites in her hometown of Fort Myers on the west coast of Florida. Some of her topics include Sanibel Island's famous lighthouse; the Burroughs Home, which is listed on the National Register of Historic Places; and an account of the history of Fort Myers. Prudy talked about her enterprises:

"I attended a national convention for writers in San Antonio, and while I was there, I paid a visit to the Alamo. There was a little booklet on sale for $1.95, a short write-up of the fort's history. I knew from all my years in Fort Myers that there was no inexpensive tourist information available there. I had a file cabinet full of information at home, and I realized I could do the same for attractions in my own area. And that's how Prudy's Press was born.

"Being an active member of both the Southwest Florida Historical Society and the Fort Myers Historical Museum has helped me when it comes time to do my research. The two organizations have opened their archives to me. I also talk to the old-timers in the neighborhood and regularly visit the public library, where all the past issues of newspapers dating back to 1894 are on microfilm.

"When I start a book project, I run a little ad in the paper asking for information, or I generate a press release announcing the new book. I ask people to share their memories and photographs with me.

"After I'm finished writing, I do the layout on my computer using a desktop publishing package. Then I take the camera-ready copy to my local printer and pay him for the printing, paper, folding, collating, and stapling. My cost runs between fifty and seventy-five cents per copy.

"I sell the booklets at a wholesale price of $1.50 per copy to bookstores, museums, and other tourist attraction gift shops. Or, I acquire a mailing list of selected markets and send out samples. I generally sell between fifty and a hundred booklets a month.

"I've also been contacted by various organizations to write

pamphlets and booklets for them on topics of their own choosing, for which I am paid a set rate. And, in addition to a booklet and map I put together for a historic walking tour enterprise, I've coauthored three full-length books published by Donning: *A Pictorial History of Lee County*, *Pages from the Past*, and *Historic Fort Myers*."

Prudy also gave talks on local history to different civic organizations and clubs and acted as a tour guide for an occasional historic cruise or bus tour. Her fees ranged from free, with the opportunity to sell her booklets, to $200.

What It's Like to Be a Newspaper Columnist

Cookie O'Brien, a longtime resident of St. Augustine, Florida, and information officer for the city's preservation board, also started a sideline. She wrote a frequent column for her local newspaper, delving into the private lives of historic figures from her region. In true soap-opera fashion, which fascinated her readers, she reported the loves and scandals, adventures and tragedies that surrounded early St. Augustine inhabitants.

How to Get Started

Writers can duplicate both Prudy's and Cookie's accomplishments by writing and disseminating local historic tidbits and covering characters and events from their own regions. After a trip to the public library, try writing a few sample booklets or columns, then approach museum gift shops, bookstores, civic groups, or your local editor with a query letter, phone call, or visit.

Writing Historical Novels

On a much larger scale, requiring higher degrees of skill and perseverance, writers have been entertaining readers throughout the years with epic forays into historical fiction. Imaginary characters are interwoven with real events and places; romance, pathos, and mystery often play a large part in the action. The author's research skills and attention to authentic detail (among other things) are what can make or break a potential sale to a publisher. Our hero can't be posing for photographs before the camera was invented or wearing a style of clothing that didn't come into fashion for fifty years. You may be familiar with the names of two very popular and successful authors in the genre—Victoria Holt and Norah Lofts. Their books are mass marketed, and many people have seen them or are familiar with ads and reviews about them.

Some of the best-known historical fiction writers of the last hundred years, and their most famous books, include:

- Jean M. Auel, *Clan of the Cave Bear*
- Willa Cather, *Death Comes for the Archbishop*
- James Clavell, *Shogun*
- E. L. Doctorow, *Ragtime*
- A. B. Guthrie Jr., *The Big Sky*
- Alex Haley, *Roots*
- Takashi Matsuoka, *Cloud of Sparrows*
- James Michener, *Hawaii*
- Margaret Mitchell, *Gone with the Wind*

More recently, *Booklist* magazine named the following historical novels as the "Best Historical Fiction of 2008":

- *Christ the Lord: The Road to Cana*, by Anne Rice
- *Come with Me to Babylon*, by Paul M. Levitt
- *Consequences*, by Penelope Lively
- *Fellow Travelers*, by Thomas Mallon
- *Foreigners*, by Caryl Phillips
- *Johnny One-Eye*, by Jerome Charyn
- *People of the Book*, by Geraldine Brooks
- *The Reavers*, by George MacDonald Fraser
- *Redemption Falls*, by Joseph O'Connor
- *The Seventh Well*, by Fred Wander

What It's Like to Write Historical Coffee-Table Books

Coffee-table books are so named because they are handsomely designed volumes intended to be kept on display, rather than tucked away on a bookshelf. They usually focus on a particular topic and are illustrated by beautiful photographs. History is a common source for subject matter, from the events of the past to the objects, structures, and cultures left behind.

Michael Larsen and Elizabeth Pomada, successful literary agents and authors, moved from New York and set up shop in San Francisco in the early 1970s. While their agency was still in its infancy, Michael took a part-time job as a taxi driver and got a chance to explore their adopted city in depth. In the process, he discovered a rich treasure of American craft work: fanciful Victorian houses. His reaction was typical of any savvy literary agent and history lover.

"Seeing those glorious houses bathed in golden California light—I knew there had to be a book in it," Michael explains.

So far, there have been six books in it. The series documents Victorian architecture in San Francisco and across the country.

The term *Painted Lady*, now used generically to describe a multicolored Victorian home, was coined by Elizabeth and Michael in their first book, *Painted Ladies: San Francisco's Resplendent Victorians*. The phrase has gone a long way toward saving many Victorian homes from the wrecking ball.

"Houses of historic value, often in neighborhoods that had seen better days, were being torn down all across America," Elizabeth explains. "Someone needed to call attention to the problem—to tell people that these homes often qualified for federal loans and that they could be given a face-lift with a new coat of paint."

The use of contrasting colors brings out the ruffles, flourishes, and other fairy-tale features common to many Victorian homes but that have been hidden under years of neglect and layers of white paint. Typical Victorian colors encompass a polychrome rainbow and include raspberry, plum, rose, grape, clay pink, pewter, lime green, and gold. The authors write in their introduction, "Because of their beauty, craftsmanship, inexhaustible variety, the quality of materials that went into them, and their sheer numbers, Victorians are the greatest gift of America's architectural heritage."

Painted Ladies: San Francisco's Resplendent Victorians sparked what is now thought of as a color revolution. Since 1978, when the book was published, this colorist movement has spread from San Francisco to cities throughout the country. The book has become a mainstay for a network of Victorian home owners, preservationists, historians, architects, craftspeople, city planners, and magazine publishers, and it prompted an ongoing surge in revitalizing Victorian homes. The second book of the series, *Daughters of Painted Ladies*, covers this new generation of homes in six geographical regions. It instructs home owners on how to create their own Painted Ladies, offers suggestions for saving derelict Victorian structures, and lists valuable resources such as national preservation organizations, books, magazines, color consultants, and suppliers.

The sixth in the series, *America's Painted Ladies*, is a tribute to history, color, and architecture. Elizabeth and Michael have also coauthored another book about Artistic License, a Bay-Area guild that is revitalizing Victorian crafts.

Both Michael and Elizabeth are extremely proud of their roles in preserving an important facet of America's architectural heritage.

Photography

Many writers team up with photographers, as Michael Larsen and Elizabeth Pomada did for several of their Painted Ladies books. But photographers with writing and/or marketing skills—and a focused project—can set out on their own to capture America's heritage.

In addition to colorful Victorian houses, the intricate iron balconies in New Orleans's French Quarter and the stately doors and town houses of historic Boston have all been preserved by cameras. The resulting photographs have been reproduced as postcards, posters, greeting cards, calendars, and coffee-table books.

Here are a few other suggestions. By exploring in your own neighborhood or traveling through the country, you can add to the list.

- Historic forts
- Early trains
- Old sailing vessels
- Vintage clothing and costumes
- Civil War battle sites
- Art deco architecture and neon displays
- Living history museums
- Antique collections and collectibles
- Shaker furniture
- Victorian crafts

Photography is an essential element in many history-related fields. Photographers are often employed by archaeologists, restoration architects, and museum collection managers. Photographic possibilities are endless, limited only by your imagination.

Marketing Your Work

Photographers with digital equipment and printing facilities can publish their own postcards, posters, and calendars for minimal costs. Approaching bookstores and gift shops in the region your work covers can result in consignment arrangements or outright sales.

Professional distribution becomes necessary for larger projects with more national or international market potential. *Literary Market Place*, or LMP, a volume readily available in the reference departments of most large libraries, lists distributors and the products they handle.

Greeting card companies are always on the lookout for interesting art. *Photographer's Market* and *Writer's Market* are annual directories that list galleries, publishers, greeting card and calendar producers, and other potential markets for your work. These books also contain articles that describe how best to approach these markets.

Proposing a Coffee-Table Book. A coffee-table book with color photographs is a much more expensive undertaking—and probably beyond the personal budget of most photographers and writers. Proposing your idea to a publisher is usually the best way to go.

Michael Larsen, in addition to his Painted Ladies series, is the author of a definitive book on the subject of book proposals. Appropriately titled *How to Write a Book Proposal*, it provides detailed instruction on how to create a successful proposal, including nine criteria for judging your own idea, eight things editors look for, and how to submit illustrations. The book is published by Writer's Digest Books. Even with the most carefully crafted proposal, however, you most likely will receive some rejections. Photo books are expensive to produce, and publishers will carefully consider the cost involved, the markets, and the potential for sales.

Michael and Elizabeth, even as established literary agents, had difficulty at first convincing a publisher to take on their Painted Ladies project. Some publishers felt that the authors' first book, which covered only San Francisco, was too regional in scope and wouldn't sell enough copies to make it profitable. Finally, one publisher showed serious interest.

An editor from Dutton made a trip to San Francisco and was immediately captivated by the idea. Six books later, and with hundreds of thousands of copies in print, the Painted Ladies series continues the movement in Victorian restoration.

If your idea is solid, the quality of your work is exceptional, and you don't give up easily (it took Michael and Elizabeth a year and a half to find their enthusiastic editor), approaching publishers can eventually pay off.

······································

For More Information

America's Painted Ladies: The Ultimate Celebration of Our Victorians, by Elizabeth Pomada and Michael Larsen. Photographs by Douglas Keister (New York: Dutton Studio Books, 1994).

How to Write a Book Proposal, 3rd ed., by Michael Larsen (Cincinnati, OH: Writer's Digest Books, 2004).

The Literary Market Place (New York: R. R. Bowker, annual).

Photographer's Market (Cincinnati, OH: Writer's Digest Books, annual).

Writer's Market (Cincinnati, OH: Writer's Digest Books, annual).

CHAPTER NINE

The Self-Employed History Buff

Profiting from the Past

Business-minded history buffs who want to be their own bosses and pursue their love of history have successfully ventured into a variety of entrepreneurial endeavors. In doing so, they've established businesses satisfying their own interests and fulfilling the career needs of other history buffs.

History Buffs as Entrepreneurs

In this chapter, you will meet a horse-drawn carriage tour operator in Charleston, South Carolina; an antiques and collectibles dealer in Ithaca, New York; an auctioneer from Athens, Pennsylvania; a vintage clothing expert in Fort Lauderdale, Florida; and the proprietors of a historic inn on Nantucket Island.

What It's Like to Be a Carriage Tour Operator

"There's nothing better than a good mule; there's nothing worse than a bad one," said Tom Doyle, owner of Palmetto Carriage Works, a horse- and mule-drawn carriage tour company in Charleston, South Carolina. "The thing about the bad ones, though, is that they don't hide it very well. I can spend an afternoon with a mule and know whether or not it's going to work. A horse will go by something ninety-nine times as if it weren't there, but on the hundredth time, the time you're not paying attention, the horse will absolutely freak out. Mules are much easier to train."

If anyone could know the characteristics of mules, it was Tom Doyle. He had built up his tour business until he employed several dozen people, owned two stables right in the heart of the city, and had more than twenty carriages, plus the horses and mules to draw them.

"The fellow who began the business started off with just the frame of an old farm wagon," Tom recalled. "He built some seats and a roof on top of it. He also had a carriage from the Jack Daniels Brewery, and he picked up a few old carriages from auctions. But they're not really built heavy-duty enough for the kind of work we use them for, and they're too small. It's hard to find an antique carriage that will carry six or sixteen people. Because of that, we began designing our own carriages."

Tom employed one person who did nothing but build carriages. He also had a full barn staff, an office manager, a bookkeeper, a secretary, a ticket collector, and drivers who also doubled as grooms. But everyone was also a licensed tour guide.

"The key to doing well in the carriage business," Tom explained, "is when the business is here, you've got to be able to handle it, and when it's not here, you have to be able to get real small. We're very seasonal."

Tom moved to Charleston from Massachusetts to study at the Citadel, the Military College of South Carolina. When he finished with his bachelor's degree in history, he looked around for work he would enjoy. But most of the things he liked to do didn't pay enough money to support a family, so he was often forced to hold down two jobs. Out of this moonlighting, he discovered the Palmetto Carriage Works and started there as a part-time carriage driver–cum–tour guide. Within a year, he had graduated to full-time status and was working sixty to seventy hours a week. When the original owner decided it was time to retire in 1982, he offered the business to Tom.

"I didn't have a dime at the time," Tom admitted, "but he gave me such a good deal, I was able to go out and find some other people who were willing to invest, and I put together a little group of silent partners.

"It's possible to start small in this business," Tom maintained. "You don't need an office or a ticket collector or a fleet of carriages. With an investment of about $6,000—for the carriage, the tack, the animal, and various permits—you can position yourself in a place that's visible to tourists, perhaps outside a visitor's information center or near a popular place to stay or visit.

"It's a see-and-do thing," he said. "The carriages themselves are the best advertising. Tourists will ask the driver, 'Hey, how do I get on one of these?'" The real bread and butter of the business is the walk-up tourist.

"But to make it work, you have to live the business," Tom warned. "You have to be out there driving every day, making friends and getting to know everyone. Then word of mouth will get you going."

Tom also marketed his business to the big hotels in town and the meeting planners and found his niche with large groups. "People come into town for a conference or some other event, and they might want to do an off-premises function, maybe have dinner at a historic building. I tell them, 'Well, here's what we'll do. We'll pick you up in carriages and transport you there.'"

Tom also ran a free shuttle service with his 1934 antique Ford bus. He moved his customers from the visitor's center to his tours' starting point.

Tom's tours were an hour long and covered twenty blocks of the Old City. Drivers provided a nonstop narration about Charleston's history, architecture, gardens, people, and points of interest.

"As opposed to a motorized tour, our drivers can turn and talk to the people and make eye contact," Tom says. "It's a leisurely business. While you're waiting for the carriage to fill up, you chat with the passengers. To have a really great tour, you need to get to know your customers. And tourists are great to deal with because 99.9 percent of them are in a good mood. They're on vacation, after all! When I take people on a carriage tour, everyone in the city benefits because I leave them so happy with Charleston, they're wanting to do more and to come back."

To have a successful business, you must love the city where you're set up, and you have to know everything about its local history.

"Good business sense is also important," Tom said, "and when you're the boss, you have to monitor your drivers—the tour they give is the most important part. I occasionally pay strangers to ride and check out the drivers."

Tom was convinced that the tour business is more than a job, and he said it's a lifestyle. "You get to work with the animals, which I really like. You can bring your children to work, and all the neighborhood kids come around the stables to help out and get free rides. You have to do a good job. You're not only representing yourself, you're representing the whole city."

Fine, handmade, wooden carriages and wagons can occasionally be purchased from farmers in Amish settlements, such as those in Indiana, Ohio, Pennsylvania, and Tennessee. To help locate these settlements, write or call the state's department of tourism, which will be able to direct you. In addition, a famous Amish newspaper, the *Budget*, is published in Sugarcreek, Ohio, and a classified ad will reach Amish and Mennonite communities throughout the Americas. Write to:

Budget
Sugarcreek Publishing
PO Box 249
Sugarcreek, OH 44681

What It's Like to Be an Antiques Dealer

Many antiques dealers confess to loving what they do so much that they hate to sell the pieces they have discovered and bought.

"If you scratch a dealer, you'll find a collector underneath," revealed Adam Perl, proprietor of Pastimes, an antiques and collectibles shop in Ithaca, New York. "Many of us have gone into business just to finance our collecting habits!"

Adam's own collecting habit began in the seventh grade when a classmate brought a book to school called *Cash for Your Coins*. Even if that hadn't happened, however, it's unlikely the collecting bug would have passed Adam by. He grew up surrounded by art and antiques. As an art historian, his mother worked at the Museum of Modern Art in New York, the Andrew Dickson White Museum at Cornell, and the Smithsonian's Hirshhorn Museum. His father was a writer, and both parents were serious collectors.

Surprisingly, Adam had never been to an auction until he was a young adult. He had just rented an unfurnished apartment when he found out about a country auction being held nearby.

"I was instantly hooked. I spent $100 and filled my van three times. I furnished my entire apartment, with items to spare. The early seventies was a golden age of buying, when wonderful three- and four-generation estates were being broken up all over the country, but especially in the Northeast. There wasn't much of an antiques market in any field then—you could buy anything for the proverbial song in those days."

With no thought of turning it into a business at that time, Adam began frequenting auctions for the fun of it. He'd go out with $5 or $10 in his pocket and come home with treasures. "I kept doing it over and over again, until I felt I had much more than I could fit in my apartment," he recalled. "I realized from seeing people's setups at flea markets that they had an organized system of pricing and that they generally specialized in a particular area, such as knives or dolls. I learned that if I took the things I bought and cleaned them up a bit—polished the brass, refinished the wood, and stove-blacked the iron—that I could actually sell them for more than I had paid for them. I had my first garage sale and made a little money on it. It wasn't much of a step from that to connect with New York City and the contacts I had there."

He talked to several dealers and tried to learn from people who were sympathetic and who would teach him. "At the time, the world of antiques was pretty much a mystery; there was this arcane underground where people wouldn't reveal their secrets or knowledge to anyone," Adam recalled.

Adam found his sympathetic antique dealers at American Hurrah, which eventually became a well-known shop run by Joel and Kate Kopp, who specialized in quilts and photographic images.

"The Kopps were very forthcoming and didn't hold anything back," Adam said. "They taught me that you should try to double your money. You don't always do it, or sometimes you do better, but that's what you aim for. They taught me how to judge the condition of an item and how to develop and trust my own taste. They also helped to bail me out when I made mistakes.

"I became a 'picker,' a term in the industry for a wholesaler. The picker, during his antique hunting expeditions, tries to pick out the one great item out of the ten thousand he sees. I would actually buy retail at shops in upstate New York, perhaps finding a quilt, beautifully made and in excellent condition, for $25 to $50. I would then take it to the city and sell it for double the purchase price.

"The Kopps had taught me to look for the fine cotton quilts that were hand stitched with good colors and good patterns and early nineteenth-century materials. I had bought a quilt at a garage sale for $4, but it didn't meet any of those criteria. It was thick, heavy wool, twentieth century, rather ugly. But still, there was something about it that was really striking. It had a man's wool tank-top bathing suit stitched into it, complete with its Sears Roebuck label. I took this to New York, but the Kopps didn't think much of it. But they were always very nice to me; they bought the quilt for $12, and I was relieved. Later they turned around and were able to sell it for $50. This quilt was sold many times and eventually ended up in the Louvre Museum in Paris as an important example of early twentieth-century American folk art!

Anybody who's been in business has made mistakes from time to time. Incidents like this can happen to the best of us."

Starting on a Shoestring. Adam opened his first shop in 1973 with just $400. A condemned high school had just been bought by an architect who remodeled it and converted it into a lively arcade of shops and boutiques called the DeWitt Building. Adam rented an unpretentious hole-in-the-wall for $125 a month plus one month's rent as a security deposit. The landlord gave him some paint, and he bought a huge old machine-made oriental rug for $1. "The rug had several feet missing in the corner. I spent another $1 and bought a big overstuffed chair to cover the hole. After the $2 that I spent on decor, I had $148 left for merchandise," he said with a grin.

Adam left the business for a few years, but he returned to open his current shop, Pastimes. "This is one of the best businesses to get into on little or no capital," he said. "You don't need any particular expertise or any particular degree. You do need to have some stock and a couple of tables and table coverings. And then you can hit the flea markets. You can still find perfectly good flea markets where you can set up for $10 to $25. Later you can graduate to a little bit higher-caliber show, whose fees might be from $35 to $100. A lot of people just do shows. It's the exception actually having a retail shop. You're tied down and have the overhead.

"Many people get started in this business as they're heading toward retirement. They ease into it the last five or ten years of their working careers and then do it as a retirement business to supplement their pensions and social security income.

"And, it's a recession-resistant business. When times are hard, antiques are a better buy than new items. People are shopping more carefully, and even noncollectors who just want to get good practical furniture, tools, or gifts will turn to antiques."

Adam said he was a firm believer that, in this business, the less money you have, the better. "I knew a young man who had inherited $50,000. This was many years ago when that was really a lot of money. He went out and bought every exquisite piece of furniture he could find. I remember at the auctions I was very jealous; he could outbid everybody. He opened up a shop with all those beautiful things, but he couldn't sell them because he'd paid too much for them. You have to develop, through experience, knowledge of what the market will bear. There's no substitute for the actual buying and selling of merchandise to learn about the market and pricing. There are thousands of antiques price guides, but this is something you can't really learn by the book. It's best to get into it gradually, go to a lot of antiques shows and shops, compare prices, do your homework."

"You have to be careful about where you buy your merchandise," Adam warned. "It's vital to make sure the auctioneers and dealers are reputable.

"There's a great deal of dishonesty in the business," he admitted. "A dealer might misrepresent an item's condition or authenticity. It's easy to get caught. Fairly recently, a local dealer of questionable repute came across a big stash of mint-condition German lithographs that were reported to be from the turn of the [twentieth] century. We'd never seen anything like it—there are certain processes you just can't duplicate, and this was one of them. The dealers were scarfing them up for $7 to $10 apiece. We found out they were repros, but not before a lot of us got stung.

"And seventeen years ago I was selling some red-colored Fiestaware, a very popular [art] deco dinnerware made by Homer Laughlin in the thirties, forties, and fifties. It turned out to be radioactive. Some of the glazes had been made with uranium."

Choose Your Specialty. There are probably thousand of variations in the antiques and collectibles business. Some collectors specialize in nothing but items actually used in the Civil War. You can take any particular area of your interest, whether it be local history, silver making, the history of advertising, woodworking, tools, lace making, or photography, and turn that one area into a whole specialty and a whole business.

"Look for an area you love," Adam advised, "and learn more about it and concentrate in it. I specialize in about five or six areas I happen to have a particular love and feeling for—antique buttons, costume jewelry from the Victorian era through the forties, 1910 postcards, fountain pens, sterling silver, and antique beads. We also carry some oak furniture, glassware, and photography. Pastimes is relatively small, but it looks like a well-organized and cleaned-up flea market."

Adam said he loves his work, always chasing after the next bargain, enjoying the wonderful thrill of the hunt, that feeling you get looking for treasures and bargains. "It keeps you excited and fueled up when you're unloading your van in the cold rain or you're stuck in the mud at an auction." Adam notes that the rise of the Internet, specifically eBay, has been a boon to the antiques business. Another boon has been "Antiques Roadshow" and other television programs based on the fun and thrill of treasure hunting for antiques.

What It's Like to Be an Auctioneer

"I have this *nice oak rolltop desk*—how about a *five*-hundred-dollar bid, get five hundred, get five hundred, get *two* and a *half*, start us off, give us a *hundred*, give a *hundred* . . ." This is part of the rapid-fire, traditional chant that you would hear from auctioneer Jim Ridolfi in Troy, Pennsylvania.

"Everyone has a chant, and everyone develops their own," Jim said. "I try not to use too many words—the people won't understand you. What they're listening for is the numbers. You learn a basic method at auctioneer training school, and then you take it and refine it and make it into your own."

Education and Training. Auctioneer training programs can run from two weeks to three or four months, depending on your state's requirements. While in training, auctioneers also study communications skills, the law as applied to auctioneers, marketing and advertising, auction management, valuing and appraisal methods, and selling real estate. In addition to real estate, auctioneers also handle art and antiques, rare books and documents, household items, livestock, automobiles, trucks, motorcycles, and boats, among many other things.

Different states have different licensing laws. Some states have none at all, but some are very rigorous with what they require. Many auctioneers go through various national auctioneering schools; the best-known one is the Missouri Auction School, which has been in existence for more than a hundred years. *Newsweek* called it "the Harvard of auctioneering schools."

It's important to check first which schools' training your state will accept. Contact your state licensing board and find out what it requires, then write or call the National Auctioneers Association (listed in Appendix A) to find the appropriate training.

Finding Your Niche. Like Jim Ridolfi, many auctioneers are also antiques dealers. Jim specialized in old phonographs and radios and had a particular love for mid- to late-nineteenth-century items. Jim became an auctioneer in 1992. He advertised his services in newspapers and made contacts with other antiques dealers, estate attorneys, and will executors.

Auctioneers may hold their events indoors in hotel ballrooms or outside in a farmer's field or an estate's backyard. They usually work on a percentage basis, earning between 15 and 30 percent of the price of each item sold.

In addition to the auctioneer, there are other employment possibilities for working in and around auctions:

- **Appraisers** help authenticate and place dollar values on major items.
- **Catalogers** work with large estates, organizing the items and taking precise inventories.

- **Advertisers and marketers** help the auctioneer inform the public about his or her services and particular auction events.
- **Runners** move the items for sale from the holding area to the auction stage.
- **Floor managers** supervise the runners, let them know which items are going up next, and take care of any other details so that the auctioneer is not distracted.
- **Clerks** make a record of the proceedings and handle the numbering of lots and bidders.
- **Cashiers** collect the money.
- **Security guards** watch over sold items while they're waiting to be picked up.
- **Caterers** provide the refreshments for the audience and staff.
- **Furniture refinishers and restorers**, while not usually working directly with an auction, find work with dealers or private individuals giving life back to old or damaged items.
- **Flea market and antiques show organizers** put on the big events that attract thousands of people. They handle every detail, including advertising, allocating space, and collecting fees.

What It's Like to Be a Vintage Clothing Specialist

Most children love to play dress-up, and Mary Ptak, owner of Jezebel, a vintage clothing shop in Fort Lauderdale, Florida, was no exception. "I wanted to spend all my time in people's attics," Mary confessed. "I was mainly interested in finding old-style clothing. When I was in college in the sixties, I would just literally knock on strangers' doors and ask them if I could clean out their attics. In those days, they were usually delighted for you to do that."

Times changed, though, and people became much more aware of the treasures they might have stored away. "Gone are the days when you could pick up something for twenty-five cents or less!" Mary said emphatically.

Mary began her business in 1986. Over the years she managed to build up an international clientele, including collectors from Japan, Germany, and England.

"Our customers are an eclectic mix of people," she said. "People from England and Japan have been buying up everything they can find from the fifties. Our serious collectors tend to buy clothes from the thirties through the fifties—Joan Crawford, Great Gatsby, and Garbo styles with big padded shoulders and lots of sparkly glitz. Lilli Ann suits from the forties and fifties are popular now, too. They're extremely classy looking, nipped in at the waist with flaring peplums. Some of our customers are Victorian period collectors, but most people now want the article they're buying to be useful—they want to be able to wear it.

"Local kids are demanding sixties and seventies garments. The kids even want the nylon and polyester Nik Nik disco shirts from the sixties; they're popular now. The kids are always a little more savvy than the general public, and they start fashion trends with their regular street clothes. I used to be able to buy what I liked; now I have to think in terms of my customers' needs."

The clothes at Jezebel ranged in price from $5 for an Indian cotton gauze blouse from the 1960s to a $2,000 Schiaparelli gown. Mary also handled rentals, outfitted murder mystery events, and supplied costumes for several major television shows and motion pictures, including *Key West*, *Cape Fear*, and *Wrestling Ernest Hemingway*.

Mary traveled all over the country to look for just the right pieces. She also built up a network of people who would keep a sharp lookout in their areas and send her "really good finds."

"I learned what was collectible from being in the business a long time," Mary explained. "You need to have a good eye to pick what people want, and you have to change with the times—trends are constantly changing, and you can't always be buying the same things."

For anyone considering a similar business, Mary cautioned that it is important to buy clothes that are in excellent condition, unless it's something really ancient that people would expect to be damaged. "And you also need a huge amount of stock. When I started out I had very little, but I took consignments then, and because I'm a fanatic shopper, it didn't take long to build it up."

She also managed to build a first-class reputation. "I make an effort to pay people what they deserve for their merchandise—it's one of the reasons I've been so successful," Mary said.

Mary's success with her business is a classic example of laughing all the way to the bank. At first, no one would give her a business loan. "They didn't think I'd make it!" Mary said, with just a hint of righteous indignation in her voice.

Mary was kept very busy. One thing she didn't have time to do anymore was hunt through people's attics. Once she was successful, she could hire other people to do that.

What It's Like to Run a Historic Inn

Many entrepreneurial history buffs have been caught up in a popular movement throughout the country of restoring and refurbishing historic homes and converting them into country inns, guest houses, and bed-and-breakfast establishments. Nantucket, Massachusetts, is filled with such historic homes, including an inn once owned by Roger and Mary Schmidt.

A Bit of History. The name *Nantucket* is a Native American word meaning "faraway land." Although this crescent-shaped island is only thirty miles off the coast of Massachusetts, it is, indeed, set apart. It has a distinctive other-world flavor all its own. Ferries transport visitors and residents back and forth between the island and the Cape Cod town of Hyannis on the mainland. Stepping off that ferry onto Nantucket Island is like taking a step back in time to an age gone by.

The "Nine Original Purchasers," as they are called, gained possession of Nantucket from the British in 1659 for the sum of thirty pounds and two beaver hats. The island prospered well into the mid-1800s as a major whaling port, but the invention of kerosene, an encroaching sandbar blocking the harbor, and the lure of the California Gold Rush all contributed to a rather sudden decline. Only a little later, Americans began what was to become an ingrained tradition of taking summer vacations, and Nantucket was rediscovered. Business-minded homemakers turned their stately houses into guest inns or restaurants, and a new breed of fishers emerged to supply the "summer people" with Nantucket's bounty of shellfish: littleneck and cherrystone clams, quahogs, mussels, and the famously succulent bay scallops.

Today tourism still supports the twelve thousand or so year-round residents (the summer population blossoms to approximately forty-five thousand to fifty-five thousand each year), but the character of the island hasn't changed much through the years. Though pleasure boats have replaced the old wooden whaling vessels, the original Quaker homes, simple but sturdy dwellings, and the perfectly preserved Georgian, federalist, and Greek revival buildings still stand in orderly ranks along the cobblestoned Main Street and the smaller winding lanes and crisscrossing pathways of Nantucket Town.

Stroll down any narrow byway and take a peek into postage-stamp-size gardens filled with flowering rhododendron, azaleas, and perennials. Some of the houses are impressive mansions, a legacy of the wealth-producing whaling industry. Others are small dollhouses with geranium-filled planter boxes perched cheerily beneath lace-curtained, leaded-glass windows.

A glimpse inside any of the homes reveals impeccably cared-for mahogany and walnut antiques, like canopied or sleigh-back beds and carved chests, many with shiny brass or solid silver fixtures. White wicker rockers grace wooden porches, and widow's walks encircle the cupolas beneath cedar-shake roof shingles.

The Nantucket Historical Association has a strong influence, and strict building codes are enthusiastically adhered to by residents. Though other historical tourist attractions are often marred by lines of fast-food stands and high-rise hotels, no intrusive glaring neon signs or modern real estate developments are allowed on the island. Even the gas stations are disguised, their red brick structures blending perfectly with their surroundings. So aesthetically pleasing is the island that American architects repeatedly vote Nantucket as the only "Perfect Ten" in the country.

Architecture and history buffs will discover, for a start, the Old Mill; the Jethro Coffin House, considered the oldest on the island; and the Whaling Museum, as well as many other designated landmarks. In fact, the entire town of Nantucket has been included as a district on the National Register of Historic Places.

The unspoiled grace of the island that is a pride and pleasure for its year-round residents is offered as a sanctuary away from modern life for its visitors in summer. Many of Nantucket's historic homes are open to the public as museums, and others have become established as traditional retreats for generations of families and individuals who have learned to cherish their time in its comfortable guesthouses and inns.

The Inn at 18 Gardner Street. Roger and Mary Schmidt's inn on Nantucket Island was called simply the 18 Gardner Street Inn. Although it is a private home now, the Schmidts operated their inn for many years. The colonial-style house, which is on the historical walking tour, was originally built in 1835 by Captain Robert Joy. The sea captain used the proceeds of his last whaling excursion to build the house as a retirement home. Since then, the house has been owned by several different families. In the 1940s, the property was converted to a lodging house with six or seven rooms. The next family who purchased the inn installed bathrooms in the rooms and ran it as a bed-and-breakfast. The Schmidts acquired the inn in 1988.

The building is a traditional square box shape with a pitched roof and an ell in the back where the kitchen was added in the late 1800s. In front is a center door with original hand-rolled glass windows on each side. A typical Nantucket friendship staircase leads to the front door, with steps on either side meeting in a landing at the top. Weathered cedar shakes (which, along with the famous Nantucket fog, help to contribute to the island's other nickname, the Grey Lady) and a large widow's walk complete the picture of an elegant sea captain's mansion.

Spread through the inn's two stories and finished third-floor attic were twelve guest rooms that the Schmidts furnished with pencil-post, canopied, and four-poster beds and antique mahogany or cherry dressers and nightstands. All of the rooms were airy; many were spacious suites, most with fireplaces.

Roger and Mary and their two children occupied a two-bedroom apartment in the finished basement. During the first two years they owned the inn, the Schmidts completely refurnished it. In the third and fourth years, they began massive restoration of the guest rooms. They took all the wallpaper down and repaired the dozens of cracks they discovered in the plaster. They upgraded the bathrooms and, keeping the period appearance of the bedrooms, rewallpapered with pastels and satin wall coverings. They completely gutted the kitchen and replaced it with a new commercial kitchen so they could serve guests a full breakfast. And, as so often happens in old houses, they discovered a beautiful fireplace hidden for years behind one of the plaster walls. Every three years or so, the exterior of the house was given a new paint job.

The Schmidts avoided putting up new walls. They specifically chose an inn that would not require massive reconstruction work. From experience, they had learned that putting up Sheetrock can get unbelievably expensive and complicated when dealing with commercial building codes. Because the property had been licensed for so many years as an inn, they didn't have to be relicensed, although they did have to get an annual license through the local building inspector.

Background. The Schmidts are originally from Springfield, in western Massachusetts. They honeymooned on Nantucket in 1977 and fell in love with the island. They started visiting three and four times a year. But when they started hunting for property to buy, it soon became obvious that the selling prices were way out of their reach.

Roger explained, "In the early eighties, property on Nantucket skyrocketed. I was in the electronics field, Mary worked in a photography lab, and the dream of owning a summer home got pushed aside because of economics. We went to the nearby island of Martha's Vineyard because we'd heard there were good buys there. We ended up finding some property there and got into the real estate business. We bought a mariner's home and completely restored it and turned it into a small, five-bedroom inn, and then we developed some other pieces of property there, as well. This was all happening while we were still considering Springfield as our main residence. Eventually we sold it all off and came back to Nantucket in a much better financial condition to buy our current property.

"We had an innkeeper running 18 Gardner Street for us for two years, but we almost went bankrupt because of mismanagement. So, in April of 1990, we moved to the island permanently and took over running the inn. Business then took off like a cannonball. As terrible as this may sound, anybody who gets into this business and thinks they will succeed by serving the greatest cup of coffee and greeting every guest with a warm smile is totally wrong. It's not enough. You have to sell your property to a person on the other end of the phone. Unfortunately for that person, he doesn't know what he's getting. He can't see it and touch it. So, through written advertisements in major newspapers such as the *Boston Globe* and the *New York Times* and through verbal communications, you have to get across to your potential guests what your facilities are. Then when they come, you can give them the greatest cup of coffee and the warmest smile.

"But that's still not enough. You have to understand your guests' needs and try to meet them. For example, we listened to our guests and learned that it was an inconvenience for them to have to walk downtown to pick up their rented bicycles. So we bought bicycles and provided them to our guests free of charge. We also learned that in the autumn, it could be a long, cold walk back from town, so that's when we made sure all our fireplaces were working. That kept the fall business coming in. Again, we listened and learned that guests would like a little more than a muffin and coffee for breakfast, so we got a food-service permit and offered a full meal in the morning. We also provided dockside shuttle service from the ferry to the inn, picnic baskets, beach blankets, and ice coolers. We did what we could to make our guests happy. This helped substantially to build our word-of-mouth referral business.

"A lot of people want to live out their romantic dream by retiring to an idyllic spot such as Nantucket and running a bed-and-breakfast. But the first major mistake they make is when they use the word *retiring*. There's nothing retiring, or romantic, about operating an inn. You have to work very hard.

"From April 1 to November 30, my day was primarily involved with taking reservations, handling problems, and delegating responsibilities to our staff of five. During the winter, we involved ourselves with marketing, interior design, and restoration. We were always busy."

Financial Considerations. The Schmidts have since closed the inn and converted the house to a private home, but Roger learned over the years how to handle the financial aspects of inn proprietorship. He said:

"In 1988, we paid $850,000 for our historic inn, and at the time, that was a good price," he recalled. "The property dropped in value to $600,000 in the next two years, but because of the restoration and the steady clientele we built up, our property, and our business, was worth slightly more than $1 million before we closed the inn.

"Our rooms were full about one hundred days of the year, and we were aiming to have full occupancy every weekend through the off-season months. The inn was an upscale one, and our high-season rates ranged from $140 to $170 a night. But our monthly operating expenses and our mortgage payments were very high, too."

Nantucket is a small and very expensive island. There are many areas in the country where you might pick up a small house or an established inn for much less.

"Whatever the value, the trick is to have an understanding of real estate financing and to try to be a little creative. In our case, we put very little down; the owner was willing to hold back a second mortgage. Another alternative is to lease with an option to buy. We did that with the property adjoining ours, which added five more guest rooms to book.

"But I would advise starting out with a property with just three or four guest rooms. It's a very risky business, and there's a high burnout and turnover rate. Sometimes the dream can turn into a nightmare. You can't treat it as a dream. You have to treat it as a business."

For More Information

Magazines can help the self-employed history buff feel connected in the field. Try *Antique Trader*, *Maine Antique Digest*, or *Newtown Bee*. You might also look for the following books:

Antiques Roadshow Collectibles, by Carol Prisant (New York: Workman Publishing, 2003).
The Complete Idiot's Guide to Live Auctions, by the National Auctioneers Association (Indianapolis, IN: Alpha, 2008).
How to Start and Run Your Own Bed & Breakfast Inn, by Ripley Hotch and Carl Glassman (Mechanicsburg, PA: Stackpole Books, 2005).
How to Start a Tour Guiding Business, by G. E. Mitchell (Charleston, SC: The Gem Group, 2005).

CHAPTER TEN

Scholarly, Academic, and Scientific Jobs for History Buffs

Additional work that may be of interest to scholarly and academic history buffs includes various roles in anthropology, paleontology, geology, and education. These pursuits require extended academic training, including university degrees ranging from bachelor's degrees to doctorates.

Professionals who choose to make their life's work in these areas may be in a position of increasingly urgent significance to earth and its human and other populations for many years to come. Appreciation of past societies and their ways of life, recognition of the biological forms of the past and their adaptations to their environment, and an understanding of the geological patterns of the past aeons of earth's existence are certain to be of profound importance in our immediate as well as long-range future. The challenges facing us are of proportions we have never seen, as we try to deal with exploding populations, multiple new facets of poverty and disease, and major shifting of climate with shortages of food and freshwater over large areas of earth's surface.

The life's work of educators, anthropologists, geologists, and paleontologists will be of more importance than ever before in the years ahead.

Listed below are brief descriptions of these employment possibilities and sources of more information for your interest.

Education

Teachers must have a special talent; they carry a weighty responsibility. How they present their subjects will affect their students' attitudes toward history for a lifetime. A good teacher will know how to make history come alive and can show its importance to our lives today and for our future. History teachers held approximately twenty-six thousand jobs in 2006, according to the U.S. Department of Labor.

History courses are generally taught throughout elementary, middle, junior high, and secondary schools. A beginning elementary or middle-school teacher needs at least a bachelor's degree, plus certification in the grade levels that he or she will teach. Junior high and high school teachers need a bachelor's degree plus a secondary certificate.

In spite of teacher shortages in many areas, as of 2006, there was keen competition for jobs. Many school systems had to give preference to newer teachers because the schools were having trouble meeting the higher salaries of teachers with more years of experience. The job outlook was uncertain for elementary and high school teachers as well.

To teach at the college level, a master's degree is required—and, in most cases, a doctorate. At the graduate level, teachers typically specialize in a particular area, such as American civilization or European history.

Educators also work in museums, presenting programs to the public and participating on curatorial teams to make sure the information being presented in exhibits is easily accessible to the audience. Some private organizations, such as the Crow Canyon Archaeological Center, also employ educators to provide orientation information and training to participants. Educators can find work with historical societies or preservation boards as information officers or in public relations.

Salaries for Educators

Median annual earnings of secondary school teachers in 2006 were $56,120. The lowest 10 percent earned less than $27,590, while the highest ten percent earned more than $113,450.

According to the American Association of University Professors, full-time college faculty members earned an average of $73,207 in 2006–2007. The averages were $98,974 for full professors, $69,911 for associate professors, $58,662 for assistant professors, $48,289 for lecturers, and $42,609 for instructors.

In fields with high-paying nonacademic alternatives—notably medicine and law but also engineering and business, among others—earnings exceed these averages. In others, such as the humanities, history, and education, they are lower.

Some faculty members have significant earnings, in addition to a base salary, that they receive for consulting, teaching additional courses, researching, writing for publication, or other employment.

Anthropology

Anthropology, the study of human beings, encompasses four main areas, which are also divided further into more specialized branches, such as applied anthropology, urban anthropology, and many others.

1. Archaeology (also discussed in Chapter 7)
2. Cultural anthropology
3. Physical anthropology
4. Linguistics

Cultural anthropology looks at all of the manifestations of culture, including early civilizations that are now extinct, up to and including groups of people who exist today. Ethnology is a branch of cultural anthropology that looks at the historical development of cultures, the distinguishing characteristics of the different races, and the similarities and differences between cultures.

Physical anthropology studies early people and evolution. Linguistics is the science of language and how it develops. The field of linguistics is further divided into historical, descriptive, and applied linguistics.

Anthropologists work in academic settings or live in the field among different social groups and indigenous cultures. Many work for government agencies.

The large professional association of the National Association for the Practice of Anthropology (NAPA) maintains an extensive website with lengthy lists of national and international anthropological organizations, colleges and universities, and related topics. You can access it at www.practicinganthropology.org.

In addition, the World Council of Anthropological Organizations provides access to the names of many groups worldwide, along with websites and important features of their work and relationships to the worldwide anthropological community. Learn more at www.wcaanet.org.

Paleontology

Paleontologists are concerned with the forms of life that existed in earlier periods. They study fossilized plants and animals and find employment most often in academic settings or with natural history museums.

The work is exacting and sometimes physically very demanding. The satisfaction of discovery comes seldom but may be very significant. In 2007, for example, a total of twenty-eight valid new dinosaur genera were named worldwide, according to the University of Bristol's dinosaur database.

The Bureau of Labor Statistics reported the median annual earnings of all geoscientists as $72,660 in May 2006, with the middle 50 percent earning between $51,860 and $100,650, the lowest 10 percent earning less than $39,740, and the highest 10 percent earning more than $135,950. Jobs for this profession are expected to grow more rapidly than the average between 2006 and 2016, but they may be affected by an economic downturn.

For more information, go to the websites of the Society of Vertebrate Paleontology (www.vertpaleo.org) and the Palaeontological Association (www.palass.org). Also look for the *Journal of Paleontology* at any large library or university library. The society lists many more organizations and resources for students, as well as the paleontology departments in colleges and universities. Additional resources are listed in Appendix A.

Geology

Geology is the science concerned with the physical history of the earth. Geologists study rocks and the physical changes the earth has undergone. In addition to teaching, geologists work for engineering firms and oil companies and with architects and archaeologists. Many also work for the government.

According to the *Occupational Outlook Handbook*, median annual earnings of geoscientists were $72,660 in May 2006. The middle 50 percent earned between $51,860 and $100,650; the lowest 10 percent earned less than $39,740, the highest 10 percent more than $135,950. The petroleum, mineral, and mining industries offer higher salaries, but less job security, than other industries because economic downturns sometimes cause layoffs.

According to the National Association of Colleges and Employers, beginning salary offers in July 2007 for graduates with bachelor's degrees in geology and related sciences averaged $40,786 a year. In 2007, the average salary was $87,392 for geologists working for the federal government.

More than half of the fifty states require licensing and/or certification of geologists, and those that do maintain Boards of

Geology. The National Association of State Boards of Geology coordinates the work of these boards, oversees and reviews standards, and provides a forum for national participation and education. You can find more information at www.asbog.org, along with links to additional resources.

For More Information

The following books offer more information on some of the career paths mentioned in this chapter as well as others.

Applied Paleontology, by Robert Wynn Jones (Cambridge: Cambridge University Press, 2006).

Careers in Education, 4th ed., by Roy A. Edelfelt (New York: McGraw-Hill, 2003).

Great Jobs for Anthropology Majors, 2nd ed., by Blythe Camenson (New York: McGraw-Hill, 2004).

Great Jobs for Geology Majors, 2nd ed., by Blythe Camenson (New York: McGraw-Hill, 2006).

Great Jobs for History Majors, 3rd ed., by Julie Ann DeGalan and Stephen E. Lambert (New York: McGraw-Hill, 2007).

In addition to reading as much as you can about the careers that interest you, you should talk to people working in the different fields, carefully prepare your resume, and then present yourself to those who are in the position to hire new employees. Whether you're transforming your favorite hobby into a dream job or committed to pursuing an academic interest, you will find a history-related career to be fulfilling on many levels. Good luck!

Associations, Halls of Fame, Societies, and Museums

Professional and historical organizations are valuable resources for locating additional information about history-related careers. Many of them publish information on grants and scholarship applications and have national and international chapters, some with student memberships. Most also publish newsletters that list job and internship opportunities and offer employment placement services to members. By checking out the websites, you will find rich sources of information and will also have fun seeing the enormous variety of historical work that is done by these organizations.

This is an extensive list, but it barely scratches the surface of the great body of such groups that exists in the world today. The Internet is your crystal ball—don't hesitate to ask it anything. If your passion is to be a curator of antique furniture in a New England museum or a historian for a small Latin American country, be sure to check it out on the Web. Chances are that you will be able to find a group that can give you more information. You may even find an organization that is looking for new employees, and you can hope that there may be a job for you.

Many of the organizations in the list below also include links to connect you to a variety of related sources.

Advisory Council on Historic Preservation
1100 Pennsylvania Avenue NW, Suite 803
Washington, DC 20004
www.achp.gov

American Anthropological Association
2200 Wilson Boulevard, Suite 600
Arlington, VA 22201
www.aaanet.org

American Association for Museum Volunteers
PO Box 9494
Washington, DC 20016
www.aamv.org
  Cites more than a million volunteers in U.S. museums

American Association for State and Local History
1717 Church Street
Nashville, TN 37203
www.aaslh.org

American Association of Museums
1575 Eye Street NW, Suite 400
Washington, DC 20005
www.aam-us.org
  Publishes Museum *magazine; maintains excellent website, including*
  "Job Headquarters"

American Craft Council
Information Center
72 Spring Street, Sixth Floor
New York, NY 10012
www.craftcouncil.org
  Maintains library and other resources; publishes American Craft
  magazine

American Ethnological Society
4350 North Fairfax Drive, Suite 640
Arlington, VA 22203
www.aesonline.org

American Historical Association
400 A Street SE
Washington, DC 20003
www.historians.org
Maintains list of history departments in colleges and universities;
provides jobs and career information on website; publishes
American Historical Review

American Institute of Architects
1735 New York Avenue NW
Washington, DC 20006
www.aia.org
Website includes a bookstore and links for blogs and podcasts

American Jewish Historical Society
15 West Sixteenth Street
New York, NY 10011
www.ajhs.org
Provides information and history of Jewish populations and
settlements in the United States and worldwide

American Library Association
50 East Huron Street
Chicago, IL 60611
www.ala.org
Provides extensive information and lists of historical libraries and
research services

American Sociological Association
1430 K Street NW, Suite 600
Washington, DC 20005
www.asanet.org
  *Has student organization; website includes information on careers
  and jobs*

American Society of Church History
Yale Divinity School
409 Prospect Street
New Haven, CT 06511
www.churchhistory.org

"Antiques Roadshow"
WGBH Boston
One Guest Street
Brighton, MA 02135
www.pbs.org/roadshow
  *Website provides calendar of programs, archives, newsletter, and
  much more*

Arab American National Museum
13624 Michigan Avenue
Dearborn, MI 48126
www.arabamericanmuseum.org
  Exhibits, library, history, and publications

Archaeological Conservancy
5301 Central Avenue NE, Suite 902
Albuquerque, NM 87108
www.americanarchaeology.com
  Publishes American Archaeology

Association of Research Institutes in Art History
Florida International University
University Park Campus
11200 Southwest Eighth Street
Miami, FL 33199
www.ariah.info
> *Maintains fellowship programs for scholars from Mexico, Central and South America, and the Caribbean*

Association for Gravestone Studies
278 Main Street, Suite 207
Greenfield, MA 01301
www.gravestonestudies.org
> *Composed primarily of volunteers who are systematically preserving historical information available from gravestones*

Association of Living History, Farms, and Agricultural Museums
8774 Route 45 NW
North Bloomfield, OH 44450
www.alhfam.org

Bureau of the Census
U.S. Census Bureau
4600 Silver Hill Road
Washington, DC 20233
www.census.gov

Canadian Historical Association
395 Wellington Street
Ottawa, ON K1A 0N4
Canada
www.cha-shc.ca

Maintains historical collections of reference materials relevant to Native peoples; French, English, Scots-Irish, and other settlers; and history of development in Canada and Quebec

Chinese Historical Society of America
965 Clay Street
San Francisco, CA 94108
www.chsa.org

Maintains historical archives, reference materials, art, and photo collections

Church of Jesus Christ of Latter-day Saints
Family History Library
35 North West Temple Street, Room 344
Salt Lake City, UT 84150
www.familysearch.org

Has extensive genealogical records and research services, some free, some for fees

Costume Institute
Metropolitan Museum of Art
1000 Fifth Avenue at Eighty-Second Street
New York, NY 10028
www.metmuseum.org

Maintains more than eighty thousand costumes and accessories, with research libraries and art and photo archives; has a premier reference collection primarily for professionals and serious scholars; undertakes extensive research projects; and offers high school internships and graduate fellowships

Council for Museum Anthropology
c/o American Anthropological Association
2200 Wilson Boulevard, Suite 600
Arlington, VA 22201
www.unparallel.com/cma

Dryden Flight Research Center
PO Box 273
Edwards, CA 93523
www.nasa.gov/centers/dryden
  *Emphasizes history of flight, space exploration, and photo archives;
  student programs*

Fiction Writer's Connection (FWC)
PO Box 72300
Albuquerque, NM 87195
www.fictionwriters.com

Institute of Museum and Library Services
1800 M Street NW, Ninth Floor
Washington, DC 20036
www.imls.gov
  *Information and list of state organizations, grants information, and
  publications*

International Association of Research Institutes in the History
  of Art (online only)
www.riha-institutes.org

International Virtual Catalogue for Art History (online only)
www.artlibraries.net

Library of Congress
American Memory Collection
101 Independence Avenue SE
Washington, DC 20540
www.loc.gov

A breathtaking resource; major repository of source materials for all ethnic groups across the broadest swath of American life; the American Memory Collection, one of many collections, unequaled in the country

Marine Museum of the Great Lakes
55 Ontario Street
Kingston, ON K7L 2Y2
Canada
www.marmuseum.ca

Focuses on history of shipping, shipwrecks, technology, and culture

Museum of African American History
14 Beacon Street, Suite 719
Boston, MA 02108
www.afroammuseum.org

Maintains a reference library, exhibits, and photo and primary source archives

Museum of Broadcast Communications
400 North State Street, Suite 240
Chicago, IL 60610
www.museum.tv

Houses many exhibits, history of radio and television, reference documents, archives of film and radio broadcast recordings, and memorabilia from decades past

Museum of the City of New York
1220 Fifth Avenue
New York, NY 10029
www.mcny.org

> *Houses collections of art and the everyday life of New Yorkers,
> including their baseball heroes, poets, household furnishings, and
> musical instruments; employment information on the website*

National Archives and Records Administration
8601 Adelphi Road
College Park, MD 20740
www.archives.gov

National Association of State Boards of Geology
PO Box 11591
Columbia, SC 29211
www.asbog.org

National Auctioneers Association
8880 Ballentine
Overland Park, KS 66214
www.auctioneers.org

> *Provides publications, member services, training and education
> information, licensing, auctions calendar, news of this $270 billion a
> year industry*

National Center for Cultural Resources
National Historic Landmarks Survey
1849 C Street NW
Washington, DC 20240
www.nps.gov/nhl

> *Supervises theme studies, nomination, designation and de-
> designation of National Historic Landmarks; provides publication
> and web information; coordinates landmark monitoring*

National Civil Rights Museum
450 Mulberry Street
Memphis, TN 38103
www.civilrightsmuseum.org
Memorial and museum on the site of Dr. King's assassination; houses a library, archives, and photos

National Council of La Raza (NCLR)
Raul Yzaguirre Building
1126 Sixteenth Street NW
Washington, DC 20036
www.nclr.org
Preserves records and pictorial archives of Latin American and other Hispanic immigration, settlement, scientific and cultural achievements, and cultural and civil rights history; provides information and grants; sponsors educational programs

National Genealogical Society
3108 Columbia Pike, Suite 300
Arlington, VA 22204
www.ngsgenealogy.org

National Museum of the American Indian
Fourth Street and Independence Avenue SW
Washington, DC 20560
www.nmai.si.edu
New national center of Native American culture and history; website features an employment source, bookshop, calendar of events, and description of research resources; has branches in other major cities

National Railway Historical Society
100 North Twentieth Street, Fourth Floor
Philadelphia, PA 19103
www.nrhs.com
Maintains extensive library and archives; publishes National Railway Bulletin

National Recreation and Park Association
22377 Belmont Ridge Road
Ashburn, VA 20148
www.nrpa.org

National Register of Historic Places
National Park Service
1201 Eye Street NW, Eighth Floor
Washington, DC 20005
www.cr.nps.gov/nr

National Trust for Historic Preservation
1785 Massachusetts Avenue NW
Washington, DC 20036
www.preservationnation.org

New England Historic Genealogical Society
101 Newbury Street
Boston, MA 02116
www.newenglandancestors.org
  Library archives, publications, and research services

Oral History Association
Dickinson College
PO Box 1773
Carlisle, PA 17013
www.dickinson.edu/oha

Outdoor Amusement Business Association
1035 South Semoran Boulevard, Suite 1045A
Winter Park, FL 32792
www.oaba.org
  *Offers outdoor pageants, concerts, extravaganzas, living history
  parks, and more*

Rock and Roll Hall of Fame
1100 Rock and Roll Boulevard
Cleveland, OH 44114
www.rockhall.com
Offers history and highlights of rock and roll; many jobs working with families, children, and the public in general

Smithsonian Center for Education and Museum Studies
Smithsonian Institution
PO Box 37012
Washington, DC 20013
http://museumstudies.si.edu

Society for American Archaeology
900 Second Street NE, Suite 12
Washington, DC 20002
www.saa.org

Society for Historical Archaeology
15245 Shady Grove Road, Suite 130
Rockville, MD 20850
www.sha.org
Features jobs and student services; includes the Americas and Europe

Society of American Archivists
17 North State Street, Suite 1425
Chicago, IL 60602
www.archivists.org
Publishes the American Archivist *journal*

Society of Architectural Historians
1365 North Astor Street
Chicago, IL 60610
www.sah.org

Society of Vertebrate Paleontology
SVP Headquarters
111 Deer Lake Road, Suite 100
Deerfield, IL 60015
www.vertpaleo.org

Stax Museum of American Soul Music
926 East McLemore Avenue
Memphis, TN 38106
www.soulsvilleusa.com
  *Focuses on history of the genre and the stars; maintains a richly
  detailed website*

Toy Museum at Natural Bridge
PO Box 87
Natural Bridge, VA 24578
www.awesometoymuseum.com
  Features thousands of antique toys; offers part-time jobs in season

UCLA Asian American Studies Center
3230 Campbell Hall
405 Hilgard Avenue
Los Angeles, CA 90095
www.aasc.ucla.edu
  Publishes CrossCurrents *newsletter and* Amerasia Journal, *the most
  intellectually provocative source on Asian American history and
  culture*

U.S. Historic Preservation Program
National Conference of State Historic Preservation Officers
Suite 342, Hall of the States
444 North Capitol Street NW
Washington, DC 20001
www.ncshpo.org

*Provides a list of all fifty-nine Historic Preservation Officers, with
links to each state's website for extensive information about state
programs, education, calendars, and contacts*

U.S. Institute for Theatre Technology
315 South Crouse Avenue, Suite 200
Syracuse, NY 13210
www.usitt.org

Provides publications, member services, and career and job postings

Living History Museums

What follows is a small sampling from among the thousands of living history museums located throughout the country. Many have websites that list current employment opportunities. Contact those that interest you directly for additional information.

Canadian Museum of Civilization
100 Laurier Street
Gatineau, QC K1A 0M8
Canada
www.civilization.ca

Clear Creek History Park
c/o Astor House Museum
822 Twelfth Street
Golden, CO 80401
www.astorhousemuseum.org

Colonial Williamsburg
PO Box 1776
Williamsburg, VA 23187
www.history.org

El Rancho de las Golondrinas
334 Los Pinos Road
Santa Fe, NM 87507
www.golondrinas.org

Frontier Culture Museum
PO Box 810
Staunton, VA 24402
www.frontiermuseum.org

Genesee Country Village & Museum
1410 Flint Hill Road
Mumford, NY 14511
www.gcv.org

Hancock Shaker Village
PO Box 927
Pittsfield, MA 01201
www.hancockshakervillage.org

Historic Charlton Park
2545 South Charlton Park Road
Hastings, MI 49058
www.charltonpark.org

Living History Farms
2600 111th Street
Urbandale, IA 50322
www.lhf.org

Lowell National Historical Park
U.S. National Park Service
246 Market Street
Lowell, MA 01852
www.nps.gov/lowe

Museum Village
1010 Route 17M
Monroe, NY 10950
www.museumvillage.org

Mystic Seaport
PO Box 6000
75 Greenmanville Avenue
Mystic, CT 06355
www.mysticseaport.org

Old Cowtown Museum
1865 Museum Boulevard
Wichita, KS 67203
www.oldcowtown.org

Old Salem Living History Museums
Old Salem Museums and Gardens
PO Box F, Salem Station
Winston-Salem, NC 27108
www.oldsalem.org

Old Sturbridge Village
One Old Sturbridge Village Road
Sturbridge, MA 01566
www.osv.org

Plimoth Plantation
137 Warren Avenue
Plymouth, MA 02360
www.plimoth.org

Pioneer Arizona Living History Village
3901 West Pioneer Road
Phoenix, AZ 85086
www.pioneer-arizona.com

Rhinebeck Aerodrome Museum
PO Box 229
Rhinebeck, NY 12572
www.oldrhinebeck.org

St. Augustine Spanish Quarter Village
Colonial St. Augustine Foundation
29 St. George Street
St. Augustine, FL 32084
www.historicstaugustine.com

Stuhr Museum of the Prairie Pioneer
Pioneer Research Department
3133 West U.S. Highway 34
Grand Island, NE 68801
www.stuhrmuseum.org

Washington Irving Trail Museum
3918 South Mehan Road
Ripley, OK 74062
www.cowboy.net/non-profit/irving

National Park Service Regional Offices

NATIONAL PARK SERVICE HEADQUARTERS
Director
National Park Service
1849 C Street NW
Washington, DC 20240
www.nps.gov

REGIONAL OFFICES
Alaska Area Region
National Park Service
240 West Fifth Avenue, Room 114
Anchorage, AK 99501
www.nps.gov/akso

Midwest Region
National Park Service
601 Riverfront Drive
Omaha, NE 68102

Midwest Archaeological Center
Federal Building, Room 474
100 Centennial Mall North
Lincoln, NE 68508
www.nps.gov/mwac

Intermountain Region
National Park Service
12795 Alameda Parkway
Denver, CO 80225
http://imgis.nps.gov

Northeast Region
National Park Service
U.S. Custom House
200 Chestnut Street, Fifth Floor
Philadelphia, PA 19106
www.nps.gov/nero

National Capital Region
National Park Service
1100 Ohio Drive, SW
Washington, DC 20242
www.nps.gov/ncro

Pacific West Region
National Park Service
One Jackson Center
1111 Jackson Street, Suite 700
Oakland, CA 94607
www.nps.gov/pwro

Southeast Region
National Park Service
100 Alabama Street SW
1924 Building
Atlanta, GA 30303

Southeast Archaeological Center
National Park Service
2035 East Paul Dirac Drive
Johnson Building, Suite 120
Tallahassee, FL 32310
www.nps.gov/seac

Further Reading

The American Heritage Book of Great Historic Places, by Richard Ketchum (New York: American Heritage, 1973).

The Antiques Clinic: A Guide to Damage, Care, and Restoration, by James Fielden, Richard Garnier, Yukette Burt, Paul Davidson (Hauppauge, NY: Barron's Educational Series, 1998).

Chronicle Guidance Occupational Briefs. A series of briefs describing each of the professions of anthropologists, archaeologists, criminologists, demographers, economists, genealogists, geographers, librarians, linguists, museum curators, political scientists, and sociologists. They can be ordered through Chronicle Guidance Publications at www.chronicleguidance.com.

Creating a Winning Online Exhibition: A Guide for Libraries, Archives, and Museums, by Martin Kalfatovic (Chicago: ALA Editions, 2002).

Directory of Historical Organizations in the United States and Canada, 15th ed., by the American Association for State and Local History (Walnut Creek, CA: AltaMira Press, 2001). This book is currently out of print, but it can be found in many libraries, and used copies can be ordered through www.powells.com. It lists more than thirteen thousand historical and genealogical societies, museums, archives, and other history-related groups.

Doing Oral History: A Practical Guide, 2nd ed., by Donald Ritchie (Oxford, England: Oxford University Press, 2003).

From Royal to National: The Louvre Museum and the Bibliothèque Nationale, by Bette W. Oliver (Lanham, MD: Lexington Books, 2006).

Great Jobs for History Majors, by Julie Ann DeGalan and Stephen E. Lambert (New York: McGraw-Hill, 2007).

A Guide to Artifacts of Colonial America, by Ivor Noel Hume (New York: Alfred A. Knopf, 2001).

Introduction to Museum Work, 3rd ed., by G. Ellis Burcaw (Walnut Creek, CA: AltaMira Press, 1997). For museum workers worldwide. Covers collections, interpretation, educational programs, and exhibits.

Living History Reader: Museums, by Jay Anderson (Nashville, TN: American Association for State and Local History, 1991). An anthology of articles written about living history by museum interpreters and enthusiasts.

Managing Historical Records Programs: A Guide for Historical Agencies, by Bruce W. Dearstyne (Walnut Creek, CA: AltaMira Press, 2000)

Museum Archives: An Introduction, 2nd ed., edited by Deborah Wythe (Chicago: Society of American Archivists, 2004).

National Register of Historic Places, by the American Association for State and Local History, National Park Service, and National Conference of State Historic Preservation Officers (Washington, DC: Preservation Press, 1995). This book is out of print, but it can be found in many libraries. It lists more than fifty thousand designations by the National Park Service as places worthy of preservation.

Past into Present: Effective Techniques for First-Person Historical Interpretation, by Stacy F. Roth (Chapel Hill, NC: University of North Carolina Press, 1998).

The Preservation of Historic Architecture: The U.S. Government's Official Guidelines for Preserving Historic Homes, by the U.S. Department of the Interior (Guilford, CT: Lyons Press, 2004).

Restoring Antique Furniture: A Complete Guide, by Richard A. Lyons (Mineola, NY: Dover Publications, 2000).

About the Author

Growing up in historic New England, Blythe Camenson became an avid history buff. Surrounded by red brick and ivy, Victorian gingerbread, and quaint and picturesque seaports and harbors, she inevitably developed a love of history.

Through her travels overseas in Europe and the Middle East, her interests broadened. She spent eight years working in the Persian Gulf, teaching English at various universities. Her many travel articles have appeared in both national and international publications.

In addition to extensive writing on the subject of careers—with more than four dozen books in print—she has also written several books to help new writers learn how to get published. *Your Novel Proposal: From Creation to Contract* (Writer's Digest Books), coauthored with Marshall J. Cook, has been particularly well received.

Camenson is also director of Fiction Writer's Connection (FWC), an organization dedicated to helping new writers improve their skills and learn the many steps involved in working toward publication. She maintains an informational website at www.fictionwriters.com and is a frequent speaker at national conferences and bookstores.

She earned her bachelor of arts (B.A.) degree with a double major in English and psychology from the University of Massachusetts in Boston, and her master of education (M.Ed.) degree with a major in counseling from Northeastern University, also in Boston.